Listen to the

Beat of the Drum

Essence of Servant Leadership

Rashid Faisal

Black Ivy Scholar Publications, LLC

Black Ivy Scholar Publications, Publisher
Cover Design: Rashid Faisal and Christie Dolar-Faisal
Edited: Matthew Ford, 4D Works
Production and Composition: CreateSpace

ISBN-13: 978-0692097380 (Custom Universal)
ISBN-10: 0692097384

DEDICATION

In Memory of the 50th Anniversary of the Death of
Dr. Martin Luther King, Jr. (1968-2018)

Listen to the Beat of the Drum

Table of Contents

It is a time for all people of conscience to call upon America to return to her true home of brotherhood and peaceful pursuits... We must demonstrate, teach, and preach, until the very foundations of our nation are shaken. We must work unceasingly to lift this nation that we love to a higher destiny, to a new plateau of compassion, to a more noble expression of humanness.

--Dr. Martin Luther King, Jr.

God, give us men! A time like this demands strong minds, great hearts, true faith, and ready hands; men whom the lust for office does not kill; men whom the spoils of office cannot buy; men who possess opinions and a will; men who have honor; men who will not lie; men who can stand before a demagogue and damn his treacherous flatteries without winking; tall men, sun-crowned, who live above the fog in public duty and private thinking.

--J.G. Holland

FOREWORD-
Where do we go from here?

By LaMarcus J. Hall

William Ernest Henley said, "My head is bloody, but unbowed". Brothers of Alpha Phi Alpha Fraternity and African American men all over this world are fighting daily with bloodied heads, but still refuse to bow to social injustice. This ongoing struggle for the reconstruction of society has been taxing to our minds and bodies.

Brothers of all colors are charged to stand up for their fellow man and pave the way for the youth behind us. As we live our dreams, we must remember our forefathers paved the way for us, whether we know them or not. We must return to our village. The call to serve is bigger than each individual Alpha man. *Enough is Enough.* Alpha men—like our esteemed Brother, Dr. Martin Luther King Jr.—must be at the forefront of social change. Brothers, our President, Dr. Everett B. Ward, has called an *Urgency of NOW*. The time is now to examine ourselves according to the sacred creed and precepts of Alpha Phi Alpha Fraternity, Inc. Brothers. The *Urgency of NOW* is to pick up the torch of Dr. Martin Luther King, Jr. and continue the fight for civil rights and human dignity.

As we remember the legacy of Bro. Dr. Martin Luther King, Jr. and mourn his death 50 years ago, the work to be done must not end until we address every form of social injustice threatening the "Beloved Community". Despite life circumstances, many of the brothers committed to an oath of a lifetime of service. It's time to rededicate ourselves to the work of Bro. Dr. Martin Luther King Jr., by working to ensure all citizens have equal and equitable access to sound education, quality healthcare, voting rights, safe housing, crime-free neighborhoods, clean water, livable wages, and freedom from all forms of social oppression.

About LaMarcus J. Hall

Assistant Director of Student Life and Development at Ivy Tech Community College

Xi Tau Chapter of Alpha Phi Alpha Fraternity, Inc.

Iota Lambda Chapter of Alpha Phi Alpha Fraternity, Inc.

Doctoral Student at Purdue University

INTRODUCTION: Crisis in American Leadership

We need leaders not in love with money but in love with justice. Not in love with publicity but in love with humanity. Leaders who can subject their particular ego to pressing urgencies of the great cause of freedom. God, give us leaders.

The contemporary context of American leadership presents a troubling picture. Whether one examines leadership in education, politics, business, religion, and even within the American home, there exists a leadership gap. Although we have individuals vying for leadership positions, the pursuit of self-interest, and not of community wellness, appears to be at the heart of leadership aspiration. This is not to say that all individuals striving for leadership positions are selfish. Rather, considered within the current of American political, economic, and cultural life, a closer examination of the type of leaders "leading" our country is needed. To understand the magnitude of the leadership crisis in America, consider the inadequate responses of American leaders during crisis situations which, in short, have not instilled faith and trust in their leaders to solve the racial and poverty dilemma. Without critiquing specific individuals, organizations, or institutions, one can argue self-interest overrides leadership responsibility and accountability to solve the complex intersection of race, class and socioeconomic injustice.

In gauging the continuing impact of race and poverty on society, Dr. Martin Luther King Jr., identified serving the common good as the first obligation of leadership. Serving the common good or what King identified as the "Beloved Community," requires leaders to forego self-interest—whether personal, professional, group, or institutional—to enact legislation and policies with social wellness of the nation as a whole as the primary objective. The "Beloved Community", according to King, is a society committed to eliminating the racial barriers posed by segregation, prejudice, discrimination, and racial preferences; and the economic barriers reinforcing racialized poverty specifically, and poverty in general.

Fundamental to King's concept of the "Beloved Community" is racial inclusivity and the preservation of socioeconomic relationships that recognize what he described as humanity's "interrelatedness and interconnectedness." King launched a full-scale assault on racial discrimination and poverty after concluding that these two social phenomenon violated humanity dignity and prevented American union.

King said it would be impossible to build American union without addressing the depressed condition of Blacks and the poor. He spoke forcefully and eloquently in condemning America for the continued racial discrimination experienced by Blacks in a country professing commitment to the equality of man, and the presence of expanding poverty in the world's richest nation. The federal government, King argued, had proven itself unwilling or unable to end the racial discrimination experienced by Blacks and people of color, and the socioeconomic oppression endured by the poor of all races.

The issues of race and poverty appear to be permanent features of American social life. Whites, King surmised, were unwilling to give up the economic, political and social benefits they have accrued over time from racial segregation and subsequent legislation and policies reinforcing economic inequality. Any number of examples can be found in American history confirming King's assessment of the nation's commitment to racial discrimination and economic inequality. Blacks and the poor, according to King, were systematically excluded from full participation in American life.

Given America's history of racial and economic subordination, King turned to the gospel of nonviolence as a social force to challenge and change the multifaceted forms of discrimination and prejudice faced by Blacks and the poor. King appealed to America's elected officials and business leaders as the first step in pushing for social change. He challenged America's leaders to take accountability for the continued presence of racial discrimination. King held them accountable for the expansion of poverty and the failure social policies to alleviate the miserable economic conditions in urban ghettos.

King wanted America's leaders to examine the nation's economy, politics, and race relations through the lens of social justice. He admonished America's leaders to disavow racism and to abandon divisive socioeconomic policies condemning a large segment of the American population to a life drudgery and insecurity.

King pressured them to use their power and influence to outlaw racial segregation and legislate humane economic policies. There is a clear benefit to the nation, King argued, when democratic principles and economic justice are the bedrock of society. It was clear to King that the country could no longer survive racial division and an economic system beneficial to only a small, predominately white, wealthy-elite.

Identifiably connected to racism and economic inequality is the ideology of white supremacy. White supremacy has operated in service of racial discrimination and the economic exploitation of the poor of all races. King noted how although white supremacy grants middle class and poor whites a sense of superiority and status relative to America's Black caste, but it is a system and ideology beneficial primarily to a small, predominately white, wealthy-elite.

The ideology of white supremacy and its attendant "white privilege" oppresses Blacks as well as whites. King came to this realization during the last years of his life when he advocated a Poor People's Campaign to address the economic exploitation experienced by the poor of all races. He believed the enormous concentration of wealth in the hands of a few who exploited the many as antithetical to democratic principles and economic justice.

Enduring faith in American democratic principles, compelled King to give *prophetic voice* to the voiceless; leadership to the invisible and marginalized; and hope to the economically disinherited. In the wake of the historic March on Washington of 1963, King questioned America's commitment to eliminating racial injustice and economic inequality. The persistence of racism, as King noted, presented a serious challenge to the hopes of the nation to realize its potential for brotherhood and peace.

Racism, according to King, was an overshadowing problem which served to hamper the formation of solutions derived from the collective engagement of both Whites and Blacks. Unfortunately, King discovered that Whites in the seats of power were not willing to sacrifice white privilege to build coalitions with Blacks, people of color, and the poor of all races. King soon learned that powerful Whites make a clear distinction between Blacks' theoretical right to life, liberty, and the pursuit of happiness, and granting Blacks political and social equality. In King's view, social equality and economic justice is more important than democratic rhetoric.

King was a *drum major for social justice.* He framed a moral vision to address what he identified as the three greatest socioeconomic problems America faced as a nation: racism, materialism, and militarism. The disempowerment of Blacks, people of color, and the poor of all races, King argued, stemmed from America's commitment to white supremacy and economic exploitation. From a white supremacist standpoint, Black life is regulated by the socioeconomic needs of White society.

Economic exploitation is the handmaiden of white supremacy in that Blacks are valued as commodities and to the extent they enrich White society. It became clear to King during the last year of his life that democratic rhetoric served the socioeconomic interest of Whites and was espoused for the primary purpose of lulling Blacks into a false sense of security. This realization of the permanency of racism, led King to say, "I don't have any faith in whites in power responding in the right way." King further stated in a moment of self-reflective militancy:

> ... they'll treat us like they did our Japanese brothers and sisters in World War II. They'll throw us into concentration camps. ...The sick people and the fascists will be strengthened. They'll cordon off the ghetto and issue passes for us to get in and out.

15

King's militant stance is absent from the narrative chronicling his legacy. On the economic front, he identified white-hegemony as the primary cause of Whites' economic exploitation of Blacks. White supremacy, according to King, was America's chief domestic problem, but it had international implications. King argued that America used unfair trade practices and military superiority to subjugate Blacks domestically, and people of color internationally. It was from this lens that King condemned America's participation in the Vietnam War. King used his *prophetic voice* to bridge the gap between America's ideals and the socioeconomic reality experienced by Blacks, people of color, and the poor of all races.

Although King identified white supremacy as the plague of American society because of its deep roots in the psyche of Whites, he had a deep and abiding love for all mankind, even his wayward White brothers and sisters. King's moral courage strengthened by his deep love for all mankind compelled him to unequivocally denounce racism, economic inequality, and military aggression at the risk of being labeled unpatriotic, a communist sympathizer, and, as he was called by J. Edgar Hoover, "the most notorious liar in the country." Notwithstanding these negative and abusive labels, King refused to bend to the onslaught of criticism directed at him by both Whites and Blacks.

King's response to unjust criticism stands as one of the most significant lessons for a servant leader to learn. King's use of the *ethic of love* to disarm his enemy, and to transform the mindset of both Blacks and Whites during a period of unspeakable racial atrocities visited upon Blacks, is nothing short of a miracle.

During a period of unabated White violence against Blacks, here was a leader who believed in the transformative power of love. Instead of encouraging armed resistance, he instead advocated the need for America to experience a spiritual and moral revolution, a transformation of mindset from white supremacist ideology to universal brotherhood.

Although Blacks endured the ravages of slavery, the indignities of legalized racial segregation, while suffering centuries of physical and psychological abuse, including countless numbers of murders, King believed in the power of forgiveness and redemption. He believed the effects of centuries of white supremacist beliefs had permanently damaged the psyche of White Americans. King recognized that unless some action was taken to delegitimize white privilege,

Whites would continue to use racial discrimination to force Blacks and other nonwhites into an inferior economic position. King set about the task of "saving the soul of America" by freeing Whites from the bondage of white supremacist thinking and its attendant racial discriminatory practices towards Blacks.

King admonished America for being a country where children go to bed hungry while the government worsened matters by allocating millions of dollars to finance military campaigns in foreign lands. It was clear to King the need for leaders to speak out against America's unwarrantable military aggression in Vietnam, and to hold the government accountable for its millions of economically disenfranchised citizens. As King reflected on the impoverished conditions he witnessed in his travels in America's urban centers, he prophesized the nation's pending judgement if it failed to address poverty. He stated:

> America is going to hell if we don't use her vast resources to end poverty and make it possible for all of God's children to have the basic necessities of life.

Though deeply committed to ending all forms of racial discrimination, King became increasingly concerned with both domestic and global poverty.

He spoke out against poverty, more specifically, racialized-poverty, as chaining millions of people to a life of hunger and hopelessness.

King believed American leaders' silence on poverty desecrated democratic principles and discredited America's position as the leading country in the world. It is of utmost importance to keep in mind King situated economic injustice within the context of white supremacy. According to King, Whites use monopolies of business and resource ownership, along with control of politics, government, law, and law enforcement to maintain Black socioeconomic subordination.

King eschewed both violent protest and warfare. As noted by his mentor, Dr. Benjamin E. Mays, King did not embrace nonviolence out of cowardice or expediency. He genuinely believed violence as self-defeating, inevitably leading to what he stated as "co-annihilation." King asserted: "It is no longer a choice between violence and nonviolence. It is either nonviolence or nonexistence." His prescient criticism of the Vietnam War provoked condemnation from both Blacks and Whites, because at the time, few prominent leaders were courageous enough to take an anti-war stance.

King stood alone in his denunciation of America's participation in the Vietnam War. On April 4, 1967, in front of a packed crowd at Riverside Church in Harlem, he called the war "an enemy of the poor." After summing up its effect on diverting funds that could be used to alleviate the impoverished conditions in America's ghettos, King ramped up his criticism of America's elected officials as being morally complicit in the murder of darker men, women and children in an unjust war.

King was denounced as "unpatriotic" for his unwillingness to remain silent on the war issue. Hidden by the outraged opposition of those who opposed America's involvement in Vietnam is the fact the war-effort was borne disproportionately by Blacks and the poor. This explains why King called the war both racist and elitist. For example, although Black men made up 11% of the American population, they were 12.6% of the soldiers fighting on the front-lines in Vietnam. White privilege enabled White men to escape the carnage and death surely awaiting them in Vietnam. For instance, many White males avoided the draft by enrolling in college to obtain deferments from military service. Also, many middle- and upper class White men fulfilled their military obligation by joining the Army Reserve or the National

Guard. As a result, over 60% of all eligible Black men were drafted, in contrast to 35% of eligible White men.

It is one thing to point out American racism in its various manifestations; it is something altogether different to speak out against it. While numerous Black leaders sided with America's involvement in Vietnam, or opted to remain silent for political reasons, King stood alone in this major challenge to governmental sanction of what many believed to be an unjust war.

King stood firm in his advocacy of nonviolence, both domestically and internationally. He could not campaign for nonviolence in the fight against racial segregation, and then advocate for violence in fighting an "unjust war" against a darker race in a foreign land. King's mentor, Dr. Benjamin E. Mays noted that King faced his leadership dilemma with conviction, courage and firm commitment to his moral vision. Mays stated:

> He believed with all his heart, mind, and soul that the way to peace and brotherhood is through non-violence, love and suffering. He was severely criticized for his opposition to the war in Vietnam. It must be said, however, that

one could hardly expect a prophet of Doctor King's commitments to advocate nonviolence at home and violence in Vietnam. Non-violence to King was a total commitment not only in solving the problems of race in the United States, but in solving problems in the world.

Mays suggests that America failed to understand the depth of King's commitment to nonviolent resistance, and by attempting to ostracize him by silencing his voice, instead, galvanized the anti-war movement. During a speech delivered at Riverside Church in 1967, King courageously expressed his firm opposition to the Vietnam:

> It would be very inconsistent of me to teach and preach nonviolence in this situation and then applauded violence when thousands of thousands of people, both adults and children, are being maimed and mutilated and many killed in this way.

From King's perspective, America's leaders faced a moral quandary. He questioned how America's elected officials could denounce violent protest in urban ghettos, while using military force in Vietnam. He urged America to rethink its position on the use of violence as conflict resolution.

King surmised that Whites considered America a White country and marked Blacks as nonmembers. Therefore, Blacks use of violence in response to socioeconomic oppression was deemed as an illegitimate use of force. In the international arena, Whites believe the use of force to protect white-hegemony as legitimate, moral, and necessary. King found this interpretation on the legitimate and illegitimate use of violence by American leaders' as hypocritical.

In the last two years of his life, King came to the shocking realization that civil rights would do little to temper the aggression of an American society founded on the subjugation of nonwhites, the exploitation of the poor of all races, and the permanent marginalization of Blacks. He stated:

> I knew I could never again raise my voice against the violence of the oppressed in the ghettos without having first spoken clearly to the greatest purveyor of violence in the world today—my own government.

Urban riots, King alleged, were in response to racial discrimination and socioeconomic stressors from living under white supremacy. He stated America's major political parties had shown little interest in undertaking the challenge of solving the social ills in urban ghettos. Because of governmental neglect and indifference to urban poverty, King stated, "All of our cities are potentially powder kegs" ready to explode.

King interpreted urban unrest as an expression of injustice and inhumane socioeconomic policies imposed upon Blacks. Both political parties and Whites in general, according to King, lacked empathy for Blacks and the poor. As he noted, "large segments of white society are more concerned about tranquility and the status quo than about justice, equality, and humanity..." Because of White America's indifference to racial discrimination and poverty, King prophetically stated, "...we stand in the position of having recurrences of violence and riots over and over again."

Political oppression and socioeconomic neglect of Blacks America' urban centers, according to King, was at the heart of urban unrest. The year before King's death in 1968, America was riddled with over 100 riots across the nation, including one of the deadliest riots taking place in Detroit. King identified the underlying and proximate causes as racial discrimination and poverty. He noted how racism and poverty worked in tandem, with the consequence being the permanent disparagement and disadvantage of Blacks.

King asserted the multitude of socioeconomic problems endured by urban Blacks as expressions of white supremacy. Problems such as affordable housing, low-wages, lack of job opportunities, police brutality, inferior education, crumbling, dilapidated infrastructure, and poor social services were outcomes of racial discrimination and economic exploitation.

As King's moral vision matured, he began to link the oppression experienced by Blacks, nonwhites, and the poor of all races to global oppressiveness of white-hegemony. King specifically targeted global capitalism and military aggression as the primary culprits.

King explained Black social rebellions in America's urban centers, the anticolonial revolts in Africa, and the global uprisings of the oppressed in Asia as one in the same. He believed racism had been internalized and institutionalized by Whites both in America and internationally to the point of being a regulative force in their relations to Blacks and those classified as nonwhite. In other words, King believed Whites—as a collective—were committed to the permanent subjugation of Blacks and nonwhites.

Here is the foundation for understanding why King said riots, revolts and uprisings were the "language of the oppressed." Blacks and nonwhites, from King's perspective, used collective violence to resist and draw attention to socioeconomic oppression. King stated:

> I think that we've got to see that a riot is the language of the unheard. And, what is it that America has failed to hear that the economic plight of the Negro has worsened over the last few years.

King criticized America's decision to waste millions of dollars in a protracted, costly, unjust conflict in a foreign land, while millions of its own citizens drowned in poverty and hopelessness. Although King attempted to rationalize the collective violence of Blacks trapped in economically depressed ghettos, he never swayed from his belief in nonviolent protest. He stated:

> The mood of the Negro community is one of urgency, one of saying that we aren't going to wait ... We've waited too long. So that I would say that every summer we're going to have this kind of vigorous protest. My hope is that it will be non-violent. I would hope that we can avoid riots because riots are self-defeating and self-destructive.

Although King spoke out against urban riots and its attendant violence and destruction of property, he interpreted the actions of rioters as reactionary responses to the failure of America's leadership to address longstanding patterns of racial discrimination and economic exploitation. In summary, King attempted to humanize the rioters in contrast to mainstream reporting characterizing the rioters as criminals. To this point, King stated:

> Urban riots must now be recognized as durable social phenomena. They may be deplored, but they are here and should be understood. Urban riots are a special form of violence. They are not insurrections. The rioters are not seeking seize territory or to attain control of institutions. They are mainly intended to shock the white community. They are a distorted form of social protest.

King attempted to rationalize urban unrest; he did not excuse it. And, within his rationale was a pointed indictment of America's leadership as engineers of urban slums and accountable for the unrest taking place within these containment centers.

> The policymakers of the white society have caused the darkness; they create the discrimination; they structured the slums; and they perpetuate unemployment, ignorance and

> poverty ... The slums are the handiwork of a vicious system of the white society; Negroes live in them but do not make them any more than a prisoner makes a prison. These are often difficult things to say but I have come to see more and more that it is necessary to utter the truth in order to deal with the great problems that we face in our society.

Since Whites created, control, and maintain these containment centers, King placed the onus on white-controlled political, economic, and social institutions to address the underpinnings of urban unrest—racial discrimination and economic oppression.

King castigated White America for living in an alternate reality and ignoring the role of race in structuring opportunities, access, and privilege. He condemned the socioeconomic policies passed by a White majority that left Blacks with little choice than to engage in violent protest to be heard. King argued this point of White accountability:

> And I think the answer about how long it will take will depend on the federal government, on the city halls of our various cities, and on White America to a large extent. This is where we are at this point, and I think White

America will determine how long it will be and which way we go in the future.

The durability of riots as a form of "distorted social protest," King argued, depends on White America's willingness to forego white privilege and self-interest to address the racial and economic injustices suffered by Blacks. King urged America's leaders to act against racism and poverty because they possessed the power and resources for social change.

Although King spoke of the *ethic of love* as the critical value by which our nation could overcome racial strife, he was not very optimistic about White America's ability to forego white privilege to build a racially inclusive and economically just society. King believed his moral vision for "a world-wide fellowship that lifts neighborly concern beyond one's tribe, race, class and nation," would be compromised by Whites unwillingness to renounce white supremacy as its social theory for interacting with Blacks and nonwhites.

One year before his assassination in 1968, King questioned the efficacy of his moral vision for positive race relations and integration. He clearly underestimated White America's investment in and attachment to white supremacy. And, racial strife across America accomplished little to change this commitment. As King noted, America reaching an "explosion point" did not shake Whites from their alternate reality. King reflected the feelings of the Black community when he stated that "the vast majority of white Americans are racists, either consciously or unconsciously."

This uncomfortable truth born of both history and experience, led King to state in a moment of depression and reflection: "I fear I may be integrating my people into a burning house."

> I've come upon something that disturbs me deeply. We have fought hard and long for integration, as I believe we should have, and I know that we will win. But I've come to believe we're integrating into a burning house.

The symbolic effect of the "burning house," forced leaders of goodwill—both Black and White—to analyze how racial discrimination and economic inequality were structural problems. King stated the following in terms of how structural racism and inequality caused rioting and other forms of collective social violence:

> I'm afraid that America has lost the moral vision she may have had. And I'm afraid that even as we integrate, we are walking into a place that does not understand that this nation

> needs to be deeply concerned with the plight of the poor and disenfranchised. Until we commit ourselves to ensuring that the underclass is given justice and opportunity, we will continue to perpetuate the anger and violence that tears the soul of this nation. I fear I am integrating my people into a burning house.

After more than a decade of struggle against racism and poverty, a distraught and tired King was steadfast in his conviction to save the soul of America.

Even as King languished under the weight of depression resulting from the adverse political reaction to his stance against poverty, he never lost hope in America's ability for redemption. King stated that we must "Become the firemen" and "Let's not stand by and let the house burn." Unfortunately, a week after making this bold pronouncement solidifying his commitment to "save the soul of White America," King was assassinated. His murder reminds contemporary leaders that centuries of racial discrimination and economic exploitation remain painfully eradicable. Given the continuing vitality of both, King expressed the need to question the entire American social structure. He stated.

> Now, when I say question the whole society, it
> means ultimately coming to see that the
> problem of racism, the problem of economic
> exploitation, and the problem of war are all
> tied together.

King's criticism of white supremacy was through the lens of Judeo-Christianity. Like his mentor, Dr. Benjamin E. Mays, he believed in the inherent dignity, value and worth of every human being. King came to realize during the last year of his life that the fight against racial discrimination and economic exploitation was rooted in something for more sinister than Jim Crow laws and racist economic policies. King asserted that White America suffered from a *neurotic disorder* due to centuries of white supremacist thinking.

King defined white supremacy as a spiritual and moral sickness that produced racism, poverty, and warfare. Thus, as King noted, "the soul of America" needed redemption from the falsities and lies derived from white supremacist ideology. America's unwillingness to treat Blacks as full citizens, King surmised, was the result of the nation's "moral sickness" And, he felt that America's "moral sickness" must generate "moral disquiet" in its leadership.

For King, "moral disquiet" means the presence of leaders explicitly dissatisfied with racial discrimination, economic disparities, and violence. As a minister and social activist, King had to philosophically resolve spiritual values and moral principles with the socioeconomic and political realities of white supremacy. He also concluded that America needed leaders with courage to speak out more forcefully against all forms of social oppression. He stated: "I came to conclusion that I could no longer remain silent about an issue that was destroying the soul of our nation." What did King mean by this statement? While the nation was still fixated on King's dream of international brotherhood, he advocated for a social movement to eradicate the root cause of domestic and international divisiveness. He argued:

> We as a nation must undergo a radical revolution of values. ... When machines and computers, profit motives and property rights, are considered more important than people, the giant triplets of racism, extreme materialism, and militarism are incapable of being conquered.

King believed the reversal of ghetto deterioration, income and wealth inequality, and domestic violence and international warfare, can only happen with a radical change in American values and priorities.

Chapter 1: Servants of All

Leadership is a complex human and social endeavor requiring high-level thinking, efficient decision-making, and the capacity to form, consider, and weigh multiple alternatives within a given social context. Yet, King identified the gap in America's leadership as stemming less from knowledge and technical skills, and more so from the absence of spiritual values and moral principles. He stated that America's leaders suffered from "poverty of the spirit."

> When we look at modern man, we have to face the fact ... that modern man suffers from a kind of poverty of the spirit, which stands in glaring contrast to his scientific and technological abundance

The eradication of racial discrimination and economic injustice is a complex problem, not to be solved by simply pointing out the incompatibility of racism with American ideals, and the immorality of poverty given America's richness. Abolishing the twin evils eroding the humanity of both Blacks and Whites requires the elimination of supremacist thinking.

King's moral vision asserted the need for America's leaders to experience an "inner spiritual transformation" to gain the "strength to fight vigorously the evils of the world in a humble and loving spirit." Leaders, according to King, are charged with unifying humanity under the sacred banner of universal brotherhood. But to accomplish this noble aim, King surmised, required a radical transformation in values and priorities.

This inner transformation, King believed, would cause a change in how America's leaders responded to the myriad of social problems threatening American union. In his role as a religious leader and social activist, King desired leaders who are imbued with spiritual values, moral principles and social conscience. Following the example set by his mentor, Dr. Benjamin E. Mays, King desired leaders with a vision of emancipating mankind from all forms of psychological and social oppression. Oppression, King argued, is both psychological and social violence that could only be overcome by a recommitment to a moral vision for society.

However, it must be noted, in stressing the importance of spirituality and morality, King deplored strict spiritual contemplation and moral theorizing divorced from social action. He underscored the urgency of leaders to fight to improve the quality of life for America's underserved citizens. He stated:

> In these days of worldwide confusion, there is a dire need for men and women who will courageously do battle for truth.

The truth in which leaders must fight for is social and economic justice for the nation's disinherited. It proves instructive to understand how King viewed leadership as a commodity and as a community resource belonging to the people. One of the practical results from this line of thinking is that leadership effectiveness can never be a detached appraisal from community wellness. In other words, the effectiveness of leadership can be measured by the socioeconomic indicators pointing to healthy community.

Like many Black leaders of his generation, King was concerned with the collective advancement and wellness of the entire Black community. He never allowed the corroding effects of selfishness or self-interest to cause him to abandon the needs of the oppressed masses. Neither self-grandeur nor elitism motivated King. Until his untimely death at the age of 39, King was committed to fighting systemic, racial and socioeconomic oppression.

King stated that when self-interest, greed, and "profit-over-people" thinking influence leadership decision-making, the result is institutional practices, policies, and legislation antithetical to establishing the Beloved Community. He viewed selfishness as akin to being shackled to chaos; he identified selflessness as the glue of community.

In King's sermons, writings and public speeches, he frequently asserted that racism, materialism, and militarism were daunting challenges, but fixable, with the right leadership. He encouraged America's leaders to confront the bewildering array of socioeconomic problems ensuing from this triad of social injustice.

So where do we start in addressing this triumvirate of inequality? For King, the selection of the right kind of leadership is mandatory. He believed American society needed leaders committed to serving the needs of the most marginalized. King held that a society imbibed with spiritual values and moral principles, is a society capable of elevating the socioeconomic status of its most fragile citizens. Societies impoverished spiritually, King concluded, lack sympathy for the dispossessed and, therefore, are unwilling to enact policies to raise their socioeconomic condition to a healthy status of wellness.

Servant leadership, King posited, is never vain; it is incapable of shunning the concerns of the poor and disenfranchised. King truly believed leaders must be judged by their efforts to alleviate the problems faced by marginalized citizens. The issue of collective wellness is at the heart of servant leadership.

King's moral vision for society never fluctuated; he was remarkably consistent throughout his career. The preservation of the United States as a leading nation, from King's perspective, required a change or transformation in American values and priorities—he was consistent on this point. More specifically, King asserted that America's leaders lack moral vision. He stated:

> Moral principles have lost their distinctiveness. For modern man, absolute right and wrong are a matter of what the majority is doing. Right and wrong are relatives to likes and dislikes and the customs of a particular community. We have unconsciously applied Einstein's theory of relativity, which properly described the physical universe, to the moral and ethical realm.

Tensions and inconsistencies between America's ideals and her practices have led to numerous *leadership dilemmas* throughout her history. King questioned whether America's leaders were spiritually and morally capable of accepting the stark reality that America's professions never matched her protections of the rights of Blacks, nonwhites, and other marginalized groups.

It became apparent to King during the last years of his life that America was committed to this triad of social injustice; and this realization led him to make the following statement: "There is nothing worse in the world than sincere ignorance and conscientious stupidity." King urged America to commit itself to justice or accept its future demise as a nation.

King learned firsthand how White America's alternate reality skewed its understanding of the plight of Blacks and the poor. King considered "ignorance and stupidity" as an encircling problem and as the sediment of American racism and economic inequality. Faulty reasoning, King argued, led some leaders to mistake the symptom—racial discrimination and economic inequality—for the disease. King identified white supremacy as the disease or the collective mental disorder causing racial discrimination, economic inequality, and a host of other social maladies.

One outcome of white supremacy, from King's estimation, was the production of "softminded leaders" without the spiritual and moral resources to effectively lead the nation. Softminded leaders, King stressed, are ill-equipped to lead a diverse nation. Instead of articulating values, practices, traditions, and relationships that strengthen American union, softminded leaders, instead, induce fear, cater to wealthy interest groups, disparage the poor, stoke the flames of racism and ethnic-discrimination, and make leadership decisions that diminish trust and belief in American ideals. The first and central issue facing America, from this standpoint, is the selection of spiritually connected, morally competent, socially conscious leadership.

In *prophetic voice* reminiscent of biblical sages, King stated, "A nation or civilization that continues to produce softminded men purchases its own spiritual death on an installment plan." One of the things noted in King's servant leadership philosophy is while he railed forcefully against the material manifestations of racism and economic inequality, such as legalized segregation and urban poverty, there was a thorough concern for humanity's spiritual and moral health.

There present in King's servant leadership philosophy an affirmation of his conviction that faith in God and acceptance of his spiritual values and moral principles as the only force capable of transforming the mindset of White America. He stated:

> There is so much frustration in the world because we have relied on gods rather than God. ... We have bowed before the god of money only to learn that there are such things as love and friendship that money cannot buy and that in a world of possible depressions, stock market crashes, and bad business investments, money is a rather uncertain deity. These transitory gods are not able to save or bring happiness to the human heart. Only God is able. It is faith in Him that we must rediscover.

Given the spiritual and moral challenges in society, King pointed to how the worship of the "god of money" has pushed America to the brink of a domestic war between the "haves" and "have-nots." King came to this realization during the last years of his life when social unrest in urban cities across America blanketed the country in violence, bloodshed, and murder. King identified *racialized poverty* as the primary cause of urban riots. He stated the following:

> The emergency we now face is economic, and it is a desperate and worsening situation. For the 35 million poor people in America ... there is a kind of strangulation in the air. In our society it is murder, psychologically, to deprive a man of a job or an income. You are in substance saying to that man that he has no right to exist.

King came to see the economic exploitation of the Black community by non-Black commercial interests as an expression of racism more explosive and violent than Jim Crow segregation. The relative low-income status of Blacks led King to the following critique of the elimination of legalized segregation in light of continued economic inequality:

> What will it profit him to be able to send his children to an integrated school if the family income is insufficient to buy them school clothes? What will he gain by being permitted to move to an integrated neighborhood if he cannot afford to do so because he is unemployed or has a low-paying job with no future?

King asserted how America's leaders decontextualize poverty by blaming the poor for being unwilling to pull themselves up by their bootstraps. King alluded to this type of thinking when he stated:

> It's all right to tell a man to lift himself by his own bootstraps, but it is cruel jest to say to a bootless man that he ought to lift himself by his own bootstraps.

The central argument put forth by King is that economic status of Blacks depends on the degree of their integration into American economic life. Historically speaking, racism eliminated Blacks from American economy in ways that denied Blacks wealth building. And, King came to see wealth as the primary source of power in America—not political rights.

Disparities in both income and wealth between Blacks and Whites, King came to understand, is the primary reason Blacks have been unable to secure racial equality, economic stability, and political power in the United States. In other words, King saw clearly that eliminating legalized segregation and securing voting rights would not end the social oppression and economic exploitation experienced by Blacks, people of color, and the poor of all races. It was at this juncture that King's servant leadership philosophy evolved from a civil rights leader to a *servant of all.*

Listen to the Beat of the Drum

Chapter 2: Leadership Dilemma

Cowardice asks the question, 'Is it safe?'
Expediency asks the question, 'Is it politic?' But
conscience asks the question, 'Is it right?'

The social theory of white supremacy argues for linking economic policies to race and social mobility. In practice though, white supremacy, encompassed not only socioeconomic oppression, but also racial violence as a key component of domination. For members of subordinate groups, white supremacy means living under daily threats of starvation and death. King studied the lived experiences of Black people for years and arrived at the conclusion that racism, poverty, and militarism were the greatest threats to American union. In addition, he identified failed leadership, with their lack of social conscience, as responsible for articulating a social vision absent of moral sentiments.

All leaders, according to King, face a defining moment that separates softminded leaders from servant leaders. King identified this moment as the point when a leader is faced with a "leadership dilemma." A leadership dilemma is defined as a complex situation causing a leader to struggle between right or wrong, morality or immorality, and selfishness or the common good. All leaders, at some point in their careers, are faced with problematic situations that challenge leadership decisions and actions. For example, during the Jim Crow era, socioeconomic oppression was the leadership dilemma faced by America's leaders.

> He who passively accepts evil is as much involved in it as he who helps to perpetrate it. He who accepts evil without protesting against it is really cooperating with it. When oppressed people willingly accept their oppression they only serve to give the oppressor a convenient justification for his acts.

The critical consideration, according to King, is not whether leaders should fight against social injustices, but how to do it in ways that bring about genuine social change. King asserted that social protest married to morality is a force for social change that cannot be stopped. Why? Because those in positions of power would be forced to morally rationalize and justify racial discrimination and economic injustice, which King knew was impossible

Morality is a central element for servant leaders involved in movements for social change.

By imbuing the civil rights movement with morality, King gave new meaning to the concept of social protest. Racial segregation was not only a social injustice, according to King; it is morally wrong. King eloquently linked the fight against racial discrimination to spiritual salvation for the nation. He stated, "If you are cut down in a movement that is designed to save the soul of a nation, then no other death could be more redemptive." King spoke to the spiritual and moral significance of protesting against social injustices and, as a result, appealed to the moral instinct in both Blacks and Whites.

King understood his mission to fight against social oppression as being ordained by God. Having been taught that accountability to God is first and foremost, King used the intercessory nature of Black spirituality and the cultural capital of Black religiosity to galvanize a movement for social change. Furthermore, King's moral courage, considered in aggregation with his ability to love all mankind, even his enemies, proved supportive of his aim to marry moral vision with social transformation. King believed that with moral authority, the civil rights movement could accomplish much; without it, very little.

King's accountability to God fueled his conviction to serve humanity in truth and righteousness. Throughout his career King talked at length as to how his Christian faith compelled him to do battle against social forces that denigrated the human spirit.

For King, God does not exist outside of social reality. Historically, King noted, God in Black religious tradition is deeply interested in and concerned with the affairs of Black people. Blacks traditionally interpreted God as more than capable and willing to involve himself in their struggle against racial oppression. More importantly, King attested that God's interest and concern translated into holding leader's accountable for guiding society in ways that aligned with spiritual values and moral precepts. This theme of God being interested in the affairs of Blacks appeared throughout King's sermons, speeches, and writing.

For example, King called poverty a social evil that God frowned upon. King admonished America's elected officials for not doing enough to eliminate poverty. When King announced the plan to bring together poor people from across the country for a new march on Washington, his aim was to dramatize the plight of America's poor of all races. King understood the socioeconomic implications of poverty; it sentenced the poor to a lifetime of drudgery without adequate compensation.

The Poor People's Campaign of 1968 challenged business and government leaders to formulate plans for the redistribution of wealth. By public demonstrations and marches, nonviolent civil disobedience, boycotts of major industries and businesses, and mass arrests, King aimed to draw attention to need for an economic bill of rights. He wanted the poor—Whites, Black, Latinos, Asians, and Native Americans—from across the country to unite in the fight against economic slavery. He stated that the "economic question" is fundamental to all races and, therefore, racial unity was the only way to fight against the continued economic exploitation of the poor of all races. King equated wage slavery with chattel slavery when he stated: "When the slaves get together, that's the beginning of getting out of slavery." King was prompted by suffering of the masses to expand his leadership vision to include all of God's children suffering under tyrannical social policies. He stated:

> I choose to identify with the underprivileged. I choose to identify with the poor. I choose to give my life for the hungry. I choose to give my life for those who have been left out.

King's spirituality and membership in a group suffering racial discrimination for centuries predisposed him to identify with the oppressed of all races. He understood also that the most powerful source of social and political power is control over economic resources, production, and distribution. And the poor of all races lacked economic, political and social power.

The relative powerlessness of the poor of all races correlated with their lack of economic power. King came to realize that creation and maintenance of a low-wage sector was deliberate, intentional and maintained by the political machinations, economic collusions, and social engineering of a wealthy-elite. The poor were poor because the white-dominated power structure benefitted from the labor and consumption practices of a class they deemed irrelevant and disposable.

Throughout the history of America, the corporate elite used political power and control over institutional policies and social systems for its own self-enrichment. King accurately pointed out this trend of wealth being concentrated in the hands of a small, predominately white, economic-elite, had reached a breaking point. He stated:

> All too many of those who live in affluent America ignore those who exist in poor America; in doing so, the affluent Americans will eventually have to face themselves with the question that Eichmann chose to ignore: "How responsible am I for the well-being of my fellows? To ignore evil is to become an accomplice to it."

King's ominous warnings fell on deaf ears. He believed that without a commitment from America's leadership, who were able to leverage resources and influence to eliminate racial discrimination and to alleviate poverty, social change would stall.

According to King, leaders are of three types: *cowardly*, *political*, or *conscience*. He described how each type of leader faces leadership dilemmas:

> Cowardice asks the question, 'Is it safe?' Expediency asks the question, 'Is it politic?' But conscience asks the question, 'Is it right?' And there comes a time when one must take a position that is neither safe, nor politic, nor popular but because of conscience tells one it is right.

Softminded leaders, King often preached, are prone to cowardice and political-self-interest when faced with a leadership dilemma involving unpopular social causes. Their decisions are influenced by self-interest, commitments to political allies, and the money they receive from corporate interest.

Government and corporate self-interest, King argued, trump social justice, which contributes to the nation's inability to overcome past racial disadvantages and current discriminatory practices. Consequently, King contended:

> Our nettlesome task is to discover how to organize our strength into compelling power so that government cannot elude our demands.

Waiting for the "goodwill" of business and political leaders, King maintained, is "childish fantasy." Government officials and the wealthy elite in all too many cases maintain white privilege at the expense of genuine social reform. The dispensing of charity, philanthropy and quasi-reform efforts of minimum social impact, King noted, are used by the protectors of white privilege to lull the dispossessed and the marginalized into false security. Paradoxically, King noted, the oppressed cannot expect social justice from a system committed to racial stratification and economic inequality. The entire American economic system, according to King was in need of restructuring because the system itself produces the very economic inequality it attempts to redress through philanthropic efforts and social reform. Based on this argument, King stated:

> True compassion is more than flinging a coin to a beggar; it comes to see that an edifice which produces beggars needs restructuring.

King came to realize, like Frederick Douglass during the slavery era, *moral suasion* was not enough to compel America's leaders to adopt social policies to eliminate racial discrimination and economic inequality. King argued that *moral suasion must* be combined with other tactics, such as nonviolent resistant, civil disobedience, boycotting, to secure the rights of Blacks and the poor.

This idea of collective action is critical to understanding King's servant leadership philosophy, and how he confronted his own leadership dilemma. King's moral vision of collective action was grounded in what he called "mature realism." For example, King stated the following in situating the economic-status of Blacks within the context of centuries of economic exploitation:

> Few people consider the fact that, in addition to being enslaved for two centuries, the Negro

> as, during all those years, robbed of wages of
> his toil. No amount of gold could provide an
> adequate compensation for the exploitation
> and humiliation of the Negro in America down
> through the centuries. Not all the wealth of
> this affluent society could meet the bill. Yet a
> price can be placed on unpaid wages.

Softminded leaders, King contended, ignore or apologize for centuries of Black economic-exploitation. One of the most striking characteristics of Black poverty, King argued, is the consistency of resource deprivation Blacks experienced over centuries. King noted that economic exploitation, historically, is part-and-parcel to American social organization. America, King said, placed racial barriers on Black' social mobility in such a way that Blacks' socioeconomic status of the masses of Blacks has gone relatively unchanged since slavery.

King presumed that middle- and upper-class Blacks were the fortuitous beneficiaries of a system designed to keep the Black masses poor and powerless. His assessment of Black economic mobility is telling in that it underscores how Black statistical representation in mainstream America skews collective Black poverty:

> We cannot be satisfied as long as the Negro basic mobility is from a smaller ghetto to a larger one.

In other words, the Black community is a poor-nation within an affluent, white-controlled nation. Affluent Blacks experience *privilege within a greater disadvantage*. This position is supported by reams of statistical reports on the state of Black America and the personal experiences of the masses of Blacks whatever their socioeconomic status. *White privilege* is tied to *Black penalty*. Indeed, the result of white privilege is the historical and contemporary penalization of Blacks, whatever their socioeconomic status, but it is more acutely devastating to poor Blacks who find themselves perishing on an island of poverty.

In a speech titled "The Other America," delivered at Stanford University in 1967, King made note of the impact of poverty on the Black poor. The underlying lesson for servant leaders is unambiguously clear. Servant leadership must be grounded on the assumption of the need to re-educate, to cleanse the minds of both Blacks and Whites of the lies, the stereotypes, the half-truths and distortions that centuries of white supremacy and economic exploitation produced.

The American Negro finds himself living in a triple ghetto. A ghetto of race, a ghetto of poverty, a ghetto of human misery. So what we are seeking to do in the Civil Rights Movement is to deal with this problem. To deal with this problem of the two Americas. We are seeking to make America one nation, indivisible, with liberty and justice for all.

As part of comprehending King's growing militancy, it is important to gain an understanding of his perception of American society during the last two years of his life. King identified racism as persistent, almost permanent feature of American life and, he came to realize that it was more widespread than he originally thought.

Now the other thing that we've gotta come to see now that many of us didn't see too well during the last ten years—that is that racism is still alive in American society, and much more widespread than we realized. And we must see racism for what it is. It is a myth of the superior and the inferior race. It is the false and tragic notion that one particular group, one particular race is responsible for all of the progress, all of the insights in the total flow of history. And the theory that another group or another race is totally depraved, innately impure, and innately inferior.

King ended his analysis of white supremacist thinking with arguably one of the greatest indictments of racism ever uttered: He stated:

> In the final analysis, racism is evil because its ultimate logic is genocide. Hitler was a sick and tragic man who carried racism to its logical conclusion. And he ended up leading a nation to the point of killing about 6 million Jews. This is the tragedy of racism because its ultimate logic is genocide.

Leadership must break away from the traditional understanding of racism as purely racial discrimination causing incalculable suffering for Black people. Racism, according to King, is evil with genocidal potential. White supremacy is deliberately and skillfully used by some of America's leaders to influence the passage of anti-Black political legislation and social policies. This is the crux of King's argument and why White American's, by-and-large, are unmoved by the repeated violations and social outrages committed against Black people. This assessment of the permanency of racism, led King to state:

> Whites, it must be frankly be said, are not putting in a similar mass effort to reeducate themselves out of their racial ignorance. It is an aspect of their sense of superiority that the

white people of America believe they have so little to learn.

The role white supremacy plays in the lived experiences of both Blacks and Whites is central and critical to understanding King's evolution from civil rights activist to global leader for social justice. King asserted a large percentage of the White American population are unwilling to accept the permanency of racism in society.

> There must be a recognition on the part of everybody in this nation that America is still a racist country.

The source of the Black community's economic, political and social suffering, King maintained, was the result of the wealth-generating cycle of a small, predominately white, racist, wealthy-elite. Blacks were penalized with poverty and powerless to the degree Whites' were privileged by race and empowered by control over the nation's valuable resources. King understood the primacy of racism and the connection between impoverished Black ghettos and white economic prosperity. Simply stated, Whites are given resources, advantages, opportunities, and access that are denied to most of Blacks—this is the essence of *white privilege* and *black penalty*.

According to King, the reversal of Black poverty requires, in no uncertain terms, confronting "the power structure massively." Like his mentor, Dr. Benjamin E. Mays, King believed that victory over racial discrimination and socioeconomic oppression could be achieved only if the system is confronted forthrightly, with unceasing mass protest and civil disobedience.

King's moral vision evolved during the last years of his life. He no longer defined racism in isolation from poverty. Both were manifestations of white supremacy. King's focus on *racialized poverty* and the economic injustice impacting poor people of all races became even sharper as he courageously criticized America's spending on the Vietnam War at the expense of programs to help the poor. He stated:

> A nation that continues year after year to spend more money on military defense than on programs of social uplift is approaching spiritual death.

King was not interested in reforming the American economic system. He viewed programs such as job training, low-income housing programs, and community-wellness initiatives as sound programs, but with limited reach and minimal impact considering the gravity of

American poverty. The myriad dimensions of economic inequality, led King to re-conceptualize the organization of society. He called for the restructuring of society, including America's economic system, as central to eliminating racism and poverty. Quoting Frederick Douglass' assessment of the enigma of Black freedom and Black poverty at the end of the Civil War, King stated:

> This is why Frederick Douglass could say that emancipation for the Negro was freedom to hunger, freedom to the winds and rains of heaven, freedom without roofs to cover their heads. He went on to say that it was freedom without bread to eat, freedom without land to cultivate. It was freedom and famine at the same time.

In a real sense, King's demand for America to provide full-employment and a guaranteed annual income to all citizens was a form of reparations for centuries of economic exploitation. His advocacy for a redistribution of wealth was based on his belief that America's riches were ill-gotten, derived from centuries of economically exploiting Native Americans, Blacks, nonwhites, and the poor of all races, including poor Whites.

King advocated for billion-dollar investments in meaningful anti-poverty programs; he proposed the construction of thousands of affordable housing units to alleviate the problem of Blacks and the poor living in dense slums characterized by aging, overcrowded, environmentally unsafe dwellings. He placed these demands and others at the foot of America's socioeconomic and political elite under threat of mass mobilization, sit-ins, boycotting, and other forms of nonviolent protest. King's aim was to hold America's leaders accountable for changing the social and material conditions of Blacks and other disenfranchised groups.

As King noted, "Morality can't be legislated, but behavior can be regulated ... Our laws must control the effects of bad internal attitudes within the individual." He implored government and business leaders to do more and to address racial discrimination and economic deprivation engulfing the nation. He reminded White America that they gained control of the country's resources and material wealth, and other social advantages through the perpetration of both historical and contemporary racial injustices. By 1967, King challenged poor whites to see that white supremacy blinded them to the reality of their own economic exploitation at the hands of their wealthier brothers. He stated:

> Racism is tenacious evil, but it is not immutable. Millions of underprivileged whites are in the process of considering the contradiction between segregation and economic progress. White supremacy can feed their ego but not their stomachs.

There are exceptions to the following statement, but a review of history and contemporary data, supports the argument that poor whites, unfortunately, cannot perceive political unity with blacks as a source of power to alleviate the poverty shared by them, Blacks, and people of color. They would rather drink sand, eat stolen bread, and live on the brink of starvation than unify with Blacks and nonwhites to form a powerful social movement to address common interest. Softminded leaders use manipulation, fear, white privilege, and the persisting myth of Black inferiority to capture the vote and support of poor whites.

As King noted, poor whites are given the myth of white superiority to bolster their egos in exchange for supporting legislation and policies oppressive to both them and Blacks. Therefore, King stated how white supremacy is a neurotic disorder, a form of mental illness, because it is illogical for poor whites to align themselves to a system that denies them the full-benefits of white privilege. This is one of America's most serious leadership dilemmas—awakening the social conscience of poor Whites. The ingenious methods used by softminded leaders to create racial division, resentment, and hatred amongst the oppressed of all colors is truly a study in human psychology.

Servant leadership, from this perspective, requires more than knowledge of democratic principles. Racial discrimination and economic exploitation exist side-by-side with the rhetoric of democratic ideals. King drew a comparable conclusion to Frederick Douglass' argument identifying racism as the foremost culprit for Black poverty. King extended Douglass' assessment to include poor whites because this group is "used" by the white-elite to promote racism, to defend and justify racist socioeconomic policies, while, surprisingly suffering, in some cases, even more so than Blacks, from the same unjust economic policies legislated by their more powerful, wealthier brothers. This is one of the greatest con jobs in human history.

Servant leaders are proactive in fighting against social injustice. They attempt to involve all citizens in the process of establishing and maintaining community wellness. Therefore, their leadership decision-making is influenced not by racism, fear, expediency, or political pressure, but instead, by what is right in protecting the common good. In contrast, softminded leaders are less adept at discerning threats to the common good. White supremacy and white privilege encapsulates softminded leaders in an alternate reality that allows them to ignore the sordid social existence of a significant number of Blacks, nonwhites, and the poor of all races

Oftentimes, this type of leader is unwilling to take a hard stand on issues blatantly excluding a significant segment of the population from America's prosperity—opulence built on the backs of Blacks, nonwhites, and the poor of all races. King summarized the mindset of softminded leaders.

> Many people fear nothing terribly than to take a position which stands out sharply and clearly from the prevailing opinion. The tendency of most is to adopt a view that is so ambiguous that it will include everything and so popular that it will include everybody. Not a few men

> who cherish lofty and noble ideals hide them
> under a bushel for fear of being called different.

Servant leaders demonstrate moral courage when faced with leadership dilemmas that are divisive, conflict ridden, and contentious. For King, a leader's response during a crisis provides a measurement of whether his or her leadership is authentic or inauthentic. King asserted:

> The ultimate measure of a man is not where he stands in moments of comfort and convenience, but where he stands at times of challenge and controversy.

Thus, leadership is tested by social conflicts, problems, and crisis. Servant leaders recognize social conscience as central to their efficacy as leaders. According to King, a leader with social conscience will say, "The time is always right to do what is right," when challenged with a leadership dilemma. What is America's leaders' response to the continued presence of racial discrimination? What is their answer to the growing and expanding economic inequality? What types of legislation are they passing to alleviate poverty; what social policy initiatives are they spearheading to improve living conditions in America's urban centers? The answer to these questions provide unmistakable evidence for differentiating servant leaders from softminded leaders.

King set the standard for servant leaders who are actively immersed in the most important issues of the day. As a Christian minister with a social conscience, King based his leadership philosophy and social activism on the servant leadership principles found in the Bible. The following biblical passage succinctly captures his approach to serving the needs of the poor and disinherited:

> Do nothing out of selfish ambition or vain conceit, but in humility consider others better than ourselves. Each of you should look not only to your own interest, but also to the interests of others. --Philippians 2:1-4

King did not set out to become one of the most influential men in world history. His aim was not to become the leader in the Civil Rights Movement. King was called by the historical moment and his social conscience compelled him to fight against the ideology of white supremacy, and its attendant racial discrimination and economic inequality.

King, following the example set by his father, wanted to serve as pastor of a church. Later in life, King mentioned wanting to serve as a professor of theology at a college or university.

> Well, at one time I dreamed of pastoring for a few years, and then of going to a university to teach theology. But I gave that up when I became deeply involved in the civil rights struggle. Perhaps, in five years or so, I will have the chance to make that dream come true.

King sacrificed personal comfort and professional dreams for something greater than himself—the elimination of Jim Crow segregation and racial discrimination, and the fight to end economic deprivation chaining millions of American citizens to a lifetime of poverty.

In the struggle to eliminate the triad of racism, materialism, and militarism, King advocated for the emergence of a new kind of leadership –one guided by spiritual values, moral principles, and social conscience. For ease in identifying the principles embedded in King's servant leadership philosophy, it proves efficient to select five core features succinctly capturing his approach to leadership. Based on a careful study of King's leadership philosophy, **conviction, courage, care, commitment** and **competence** are leadership attributes threaded consistently and throughout King's sermons, speeches, and writings. Taken together, these attributes or guiding principles represent the **5 Cs of Servant Leadership**.

When practiced together, these five principles support leaders in demonstrating a high-degree of social conscience in their leadership practice and decision-making. Those in positions of leadership will see the utility and importance of the 5Cs of Servant Leadership when confronted with a leadership dilemma testing integrity, commitment, and obligation to the social justice. As stated by King during the Civil Rights Movement, "There comes a time when a moral man can't obey a law which his conscience tells him is unjust." The 5Cs of Servant Leadership are anchors to connect the leader to the people he or she is commissioned to serve, and to prevent the leader from drifting into compromised leadership due to the winds and currents of cowardice and expediency.

Chapter 3: Conviction

A man who won't die for something is not fit to live.

What are convictions? The word "conviction" comes from the Latin *convictio* which means "strong belief". Conviction is firmness of purpose, the most important strength of leadership, and one of the most powerful attributes of character. Many leaders profess purpose, yet few have the firmness of purpose to carry out their leadership mission.

Conviction helps a leader overcome the tendency to compromise when faced with the prospect failure, or when confronted by fear or when tempted by material gain. When a leader is possessed by firmly held beliefs to serve the needs of humanity, he is less prone to fall victim to cowardice; less likely to give in to expediency; and more likely to follow his social conscience. King equated servant leadership with the crucifixion of Jesus. He stated:

> This is the cross that we must bear for the redemption of our people.

Bearing the cross, from King's perspective, means loving humanity more than self; it translates into suffering without complaint; it means being willing to sacrifice life itself to uplift "the man farthest down." This is the essence of redemption or spiritual salvation from sin through Christ's sacrifice.

King believed the core of servant leadership is willing sacrifice and suffering in the fight for social justice. Servant leaders sacrifice without complaint. They forego personal comfort, professional prestige, wealth and status, popularity, and likability to improve the spiritual, moral, physical, intellectual, emotional, social, and material condition of marginalized people. In other words, servant leaders live a life devoted to helping the disinherited of the earth.

The *ethic of conviction* requires resolve or steadfast determination in the face of unspeakable suffering. King stressed the importance of a leader having an abundance of spiritual and moral resources to aid him or her in the long fight to help the most vulnerable members of society.

The *ethic of conviction* helps a leader decide firmly on a course of action without wavering or giving in to cowardice or expediency. Without this kind of conviction, leadership is wasted in a maze of false-starts, inconsistencies, and failure. Conviction enables a leader to meet danger by duty; to worship God through service to humanity; and to face leadership dilemmas knowing he or she has the spiritual and moral resources to meet the challenge forthrightly. A firmly held belief in God is at the core of the *ethic of conviction*.

Conviction, especially during suffering and temporary defeat, is a leadership characteristic resulting from divine trust. It is only leaders with divinely-inspired conviction that can lead the masses during times of trial and defeat. Conviction, when rooted in trust in God, enables the leader to see both trials and defeats as temporary.

To better understand King as a servant leader, we must explore how his leadership conviction was rooted in *agape*, or divine love. Conviction stems from being thoroughly convinced or fully persuaded that something is true. It is not derived from popular opinion or political polls. Conviction is firm belief in a set of guiding principles that influences one's thinking and enables the individual to see obstacles and other barriers as temporary.

During King's era, racial hate, poverty, and warfare were his most powerful adversaries. In 1967, he stated the following about this three-headed evil:

> We are now experiencing the coming to the surface of a triple prong sickness ... the sickness of racism, excessive materialism, and militarism.

King commented on numerous occasions that *agape* or divine love is the greatest weapon in the fight against social injustices resulting from racism, materialism, and militarism. His position was that there is nothing more allied to social injustice than hate fueled by racism, poverty ignited by greed, and militarism powered by the absence of universal brotherhood.

Divine love, according to King, is the "transforming power that can lift a whole community to a new horizon of fair play, good will, and justice." He also believed love to be "... our great weapon, and that alone." He was fully convinced of the transformative and redemptive power of love and love alone. And, he was willing to die for his belief in the power of love to redeem lost humanity. King noted:

> I've decided that I'm going to do battle with my
> philosophy. You ought to believe in something
> in life, believe that thing so fervently that you
> will stand up with it till the end of your days.

King's *ethic of conviction* led him to be thoroughly
convinced of the power of divine love to remind
humanity that love is the ultimate reality.

A close study of King's life reveals a
servant leader totally committed to Jesus' two
greatest commandments: Love God with one's
heart and soul and love one's neighbor unselfishly.
These two commandments represent the spiritual,
ethical, moral, and social underpinnings of servant
leadership. Godless leaders cannot lead the masses
of people. Leaders without a healthy regard for
their fellow man, especially those without name or
recognition, cannot lead the masses of people. True
leaders love God; true leaders love humanity. King
believed in divine love as the most powerful force
to transform society. King stated the following:

> Love is the most durable power in the world.
> This creative force, so beautifully exemplified
> in the life of our Christ, is the most potent
> instrument available in mankind's quest for
> peace and security.

Love answers the question King posed
regarding community or chaos. Community is an

expression of love. Chaos is an expression of hate. Leaders shaping American life are expressions of either love or hate; community or chaos; selflessness or selfishness; servant leadership or softminded leadership. Servant leaders advocate for human betterment. Softminded leaders advocate for money, power, and exclusivity.

What else accounts for King's strong convictions? His writings reveal a man with a healthy self-regard. In other words, King had a biblical identity based on his "cosmic relationship with God." His relationship with God enabled him to understand and embrace the ultimate reason for man's existence: love and worship God through service to humanity. Therefore, to fully understand the magnitude of King as a servant leader, a close examination of how he interpreted Jesus' two greatest commandments is required:

> Love yourself, if that means rational, healthy and moral self-interest. You are commanded to do that. That is the length of life. Love your neighbor as you love yourself. You are commanded to that. That is the breadth of life. But never forget that there is a first and even greater commandment, 'Love the Lord thy God with all thy heart and all thy soul and all thy mind.' This is the height of life. And when you do this you live the complete life.

King spoke to the distinguishing characteristics of self-love, love of neighbor, and love of God. Although King committed himself to serving the needs of humanity, he never lost sight of the ultimate reason for humanity's existence, which is to love God.

The service King rendered to humanity was not only an expression of his love of God but also the actions of a dutiful son obeying his Father's commandment to love his brother. King made this essential point when he stated:

> When I commanded to love, I am commanded to restore community, to resist injustice, and to meet the needs of my brothers.

King's definition of love was rooted in a larger social vision of eliminating social injustices. For him, the greatest expression of love is resisting the injustices plaguing mankind. He believed love is both a gift and a sacrifice. It is a force compelling mankind to sacrifice comfort and ease to meet the challenges and controversies of the day. In this sense, love is not idle; it is actively engaged with the worries and cares of the world. When King stated, "the time is always right to do what is right," he was noting the active agency of love.

From King's perspective, you could profess love for humanity and do nothing to uplift the downtrodden and disposed. Hence, his statement:

> We will have to repent in this generation not merely for the vitriolic words and actions of the bad people, but for the appalling silence of good people.

The silence of good people, King stated, was just as appalling as the cruel words and actions of bad people. He declared to stand silent in the face of great evils and injustices was just as bad as sanctioning these behaviors. His statement "We will remember not the words of our enemies, but the silence of our friends" captures mutability and inconsistency of softminded leadership. This type of leader act as if they believe in spiritual values, moral principles, and correct actions, but they live as if none of these precepts exist. King believed in a moral universe, with leaders being held accountable for remaining silent on issues of social injustice.

When assessing the neutral position leaders oftentimes take when confronted with leadership dilemmas, King stated, "The hottest place in Hell is reserved for those who remain neutral in times of great moral conflict." For King, social issues are never neutral; they are typically divided into two categories—justice or injustice. King understood himself as confronting injustice through his own example of servant leadership. To this end, King stated:

> The ultimate measure of a man is not where he stands in moments of comfort and convenience, but where he stands at times of challenge and controversy.

How a leader responds to social problems is a perfect way to assess if the leader is truly a "servant leader." Servant leaders are willing to sacrifice material comforts and mainstream approval to speak out against the evils and social injustices destroying universal brotherhood and community. King, throughout his career, used his prophetic voice to bring attention to the misery and suffering of the poor. On this topic, King stated:

> He who passively accepts evil is as much involved in it as he who helps to perpetrate it.

> He who accepts evil without protesting
> against it is really cooperating with it.

The *ethic of conviction* prevents acceptance of or cooperation with evil and social injustice. In this age of moral relativity, it is perhaps difficult to grasp the conviction that drove men like King to fight for unpopular causes, such as poverty. Confronting evil and social injustice, according to King, may involve making the ultimate sacrifice. He stated:

> I may be crucified. I may even die. But I want it said even if I die in the struggle that 'He died to make men free.'

The *ethic of conviction* or firmness of purpose in doing what is right is the first step in becoming a servant leader.

Chapter 4: Courage

These forces that threaten to negate life must be challenged by courage, which is the power of life to affirm itself in spite of life's ambiguities.

Leaders cannot lead in absence of courage. Addressing social injustice is a frightening endeavor given the investments in oppression by those committed to exploiting and taking advantage of less-powerful groups. Think of Jesus overturning the table of the moneychangers. It took boldness and fearlessness for Jesus, the son of a carpenter and a man of no secular power or influence, to expel the merchants and the moneychangers from the temple.

Servant leaders rely on *Godly courage* or the *ethic of courage* when challenging powerful and influential "misleaders". Like Jesus, King's courage in fighting against racial discrimination and economic injustice was derived from his *ethic of courage* or firm belief in the power of God to right that which is wrong. As might be expected, King used the *ethic of courage* when he took an unpopular stance and spoke out forcefully against America's involvement in the Vietnam War.

The term courage comes from the Latin *cor* which means "heart". Servant leaders have "heart". They can face social issues that scare or frighten the average leader. The *ethic of courage* is the choice and willingness to confront fear, uncertainty, danger, or threats because of firm belief in ultimate victory.

An examination of King's legacy highlights how servant leaders use the *ethic of courage* to face risk, peril, danger, and other difficulties. But unfortunately, according to King, "Too many people attempt to face the tensions of life with inadequate spiritual resources." What are the spiritual resources required for servant leadership? One of the required resources of leadership is courage. Stewards of the community must possess courage in abundance.

King believed the absence of courage in leadership is due to leaders not possessing spiritual resources. Godless leadership is incapable of being truly courageous. Expounding on the spiritual impoverishment of today's leadership, King attempted to show the connection between love of God and having the courage to face societal ills with steel-determination. King lived by Jesus' mandate that "Thou shalt love the Lord thy God with all thy heart and with all thy soul, and with all thy strength, and with all thy mind; and thy neighbor as thyself." It takes courage to love God and to stand up for His Righteous Kingdom. King understood that courage begins and ends with love of God and neighbor. He challenged leaders to love God enough to fight against social injustice. He challenged society to love God enough to rail against the forces dividing the community. He wanted leaders who were willing to confront social injustice head-on. King wanted a society intolerant of racism, classism, and warfare pitting brother-against-brother.

King's love of God empowered him to fight courageously against socioeconomic oppression without becoming hate-filled, vengeful, bitter, and cynical. He believed in God to honor His word to fight on the side of the righteous; he also believed in mankind's ability to one day rise above selfishness to fulfill the noble destiny of establishing the Beloved Community.

According to King, self-centeredness would overwhelm the world in absence of servant leaders. Servant leaders are the *prophetic voice* of social conscience; they are the soul of the nation. King stated:

> Every man must decide whether he will walk
> in the light of creative altruism or in the
> darkness of self-destructive selfishness.

Servant leaders, from this perspective, are men and women who embrace the *ethic of courage* to walk in the light of God-inspired selflessness.

King identified the *Gospel of Jesus* as comprehensively involving all spiritual values and moral truths leaders need to be "servant leaders." He believed in the servant leadership example of Jesus to give morality to courage by making it a force for human enlightenment and betterment. King saw divine courage as an energy capable of redirecting the spirit of hate and divisiveness.

What prevented most people from fighting injustice, King pointed out, was fear. He believed religious authorities failed in their advocacy for universal brotherhood out of fear of alienating racists. King stated:

> Yes, I see the Church as the body of Christ.
> But, oh! How we have blemished and scarred
> that body through social neglect and through
> fear of being nonconformists.

King asserted the Christian church failed in its leadership by turning a blind eye to racial discrimination, and by not speaking out against poverty and warfare. He stated:

> A religion true to its nature must also be concerned about man's social condition. ... Any religion that professes to be concerned with the souls of men and is not concerned with the slums that damn them, the economic conditions that strangle them, and the social conditions that cripple them is a dry-as-dust religion.

King made a distinction between ceremonial religion and spirituality. He characterized ceremonial religion as "dry-as-dust religion." The test of discipleship, King believed, was not found in following ceremonial acts, such as reading the Bible, attending church regularly, tithing, and professing a quasi-belief in the brotherhood of man. The true test of discipleship, King attested, was absolute obedience to God; love for all mankind; and willingness to courageously stand against social injustice.

King condemned ceremonial Christianity as hypocritical and insincere because it lacks social action in addressing the socioeconomic needs of the poor and disinherited. He was also critical of charity divorced from larger issues of social inequality and economic injustice. King stated:

> Philanthropy is commendable, but it must not
> cause the philanthropist to overlook the
> circumstances of economic injustice which
> make philanthropy necessary.

Because King's leadership philosophy was inclusive of all men, he was highly critical of social actions protective of the status quo or accomplished very little in the way of changing the material condition of poor people.

Like the testimony of his mentor, Dr. Benjamin E. Mays, King stated that he too was "disturbed by man," and advocated for what he called "maladjusted leadership." For him, maladjusted leadership did not translate into neurotic, confused, or unstable leadership. King's definition of maladjusted leadership was leaders disturbed by society's failure to address the needs of the poor and other marginalized citizens. He asserted the need for maladjusted leadership, which he equated with courageous leadership:

> The world is in desperate need of such
> maladjustment. Through such courageous
> maladjustment, we will be able to emerge from
> the bleak and desolate midnight of man's
> inhumanity to man into the bright and
> glittering day of freedom and justice.

Maladjusted leaders, King noted, possess the courage to challenge the status quo and fight to bring about universal brotherhood and the betterment of the social, political, and economic condition of the masses of people. He saw a desperate need for this type of leader and linked the deliverance of humanity to the emergence of "creatively maladjusted leadership." King believed that "Human salvation lies in the hands of the creatively maladjusted."

King is not known as a radical leader; this label is usually reserved for the likes of Marcus Garvey and Malcolm X. Contrary to the popular image of King as a conformist and compromising integrationist, he was, in truth, the proponent of radical-Christianity. Given the permanency of American racism, King's advocacy for universal brotherhood and the end of racial discrimination, economic exploitation, and warfare in a society steeped in centuries of racism, violence, discrimination, segregation, and materialism was extremely radical and proved to be a genuine threat to the status quo. King provides an example of the most radical leadership philosophy in human history—the love of one's enemy. He stated:

It may be that the salvation of the world lies in the hands of the maladjusted. The challenge to us is to be maladjusted—as maladjusted as the prophet Amon who, in the midst of injustices of his day, could cry out in words that echo across the centuries, "Let judgment run down like waters and righteousness like a mighty stream"; as maladjusted as Lincoln, who had the vision to see that this nation could not survive half slave and half free; as maladjusted as Jefferson who, in the midst of an age amazingly adjusted to slavery could cry out in words lifted to cosmic proportions, "All men are created equal, and are endowed by their Creator with certain unalienable rights, that among these are Life, Liberty and the pursuit of Happiness"; as maladjusted as Jesus who could say to the men and women of his generation, "Love your enemies, bless them that curse you, do good to them that hate you, and pray for them that spitefully use you."

America viewed King as an extremist and a threat to the status quo. Even King himself viewed his leadership activities as extreme. He stated: "The question is not whether we will be extremists, but what kind of extremists we will be. ... The nation and the world are in dire need of creative extremists."

However, King's conception of extremism did not include violence, hate, or separatism. He had the courage to love when the dominant ideology was hate, racism, segregation, economic exploitation, and warfare. King's *ethic of courage* led him to state with loving-conviction that, "Man must evolve for all human conflict a method which rejects revenge, aggression and retaliation. The foundation of such method is love."

King was particularly interested in eliminating the violent and aggressive nature of conflict resolution. He was committed to reversing the trend of fighting violence with violence. He courageously put forth the idea that love was capable of conquering hate. For example, King stated, "Love is the only force capable of transforming an enemy into a friend." The strength of love, according to King, is its ability to unify warring factions by stressing the common origin of mankind and by reinforcing God's mandate that all men love Him and love each other as brothers. King stated:

> This call for a world-wide fellowship that lifts neighborly concern beyond one's tribe, race, class, and nation is in reality a call for an all-embracing unconditional love for all men. This often misunderstood and misinterpreted concept has now become an absolute necessity for the survival of man. When I speak of love, I

am speaking of that force which all the great religions have seen as the supreme unifying reality. This Hindu-Moslem-Christian-Jewish-Buddhist belief about the ultimate reality is beautifully summed up in the First Epistle of Saint John: Let us love one another: for love is of God: and everyone that loveth is born of God, and knoweth God. He that loveth not knoweth not God; for God is love. ... If we love one another, God dwelleth in us, and his love is perfected in us.

King's leadership roots are in Black Judeo-Christianity. And Jesus Christ was his model of servant leadership in the application of *ethic of love* or agape to courageously challenge social injustice. In the teachings of Jesus, King found his leadership philosophy and the foundational principles for his social activism. King stated, "Love men not because we like them, not because their attitudes and ways appeal to us, but because God loves them." The object of loving one's enemy is not to excuse the behavior or to make evil fair-seeming. It is seldom that injustice is solved by ignoring or excusing the perpetrators. King references "divine love" when he says, "Love your enemy." This type of love is accountable love, minus hate; it is love that compels good people to courageously challenge social policies inconsistent with brotherhood and community-building. Good people do not defend or excuse injustice; they courageously resist all forms of socioeconomic oppression.

Loving one's enemies despite their failings, weaknesses, and oftentimes aggressive and violent behaviors takes courage. As King stated, "I decided to stick to love. Hate is too great a burden to bear." King believed hate was burdensome because it is the antithesis to love and, therefore, not in alignment with God's spiritual laws and moral principles. For him, God does not side with hate, warfare, and aggression. God sides with righteousness as expressed in brotherly love and peaceful pursuits. In this regard, King stated, "Those of us who call the name of Jesus Christ find something at the center of our faith which forever reminds us that God is on the side of truth and justice."

King also believed the coexistence of all humanity required the presence of nonviolent conflict resolution. He argued, "The hope of a secure and livable world lies with disciplined nonconformists who are dedicated to justice, peace, and brotherhood." King believed "disciplined nonconformist" leadership as the only leadership capable of securing what he called a "livable world...dedicated to justice, peace, and brotherhood." As King reflected on human history, he concluded that society needed courageous leaders to address the unchecked bloodshed and immorality threatening the existence of humanity. He stated:

> Along the way of life, someone must have sense enough and morality enough to cut off the chain of hate and evil. The greatest way to do that is through love. I firmly believe that love is a transforming power that can lift a whole community to a new horizon of fair play, good will, and justice. ... Love is our great instrument and our great weapon, and that alone.

Courageous leadership, according King, means leaders committed to the *ethic of love*. He asserted the need for leaders who used "Christian weapons and Christian methods" to combat social injustices. Without question, the most significant contribution of King to the canon of leadership studies is his connection of *courage* to *love*. He reformulated society's definition of what it means to be courageous, and what it means to love.

King likened the use of nonviolence as an expression of love. He did not merely advocate for the elimination of warfare and aggression; he promoted the elimination of hate which he believed to be the root cause of violence and bloodshed. He stated:

> Nonviolence means avoiding not only external violence but also internal violence of the spirit. You not only refuse to shoot a man, but you refuse to hate him." Herein lies the transcendent power of King's leadership. He not only advocated the elimination of warfare and bloodshed but also advocated a change in man's spirit. Violence, according to King, is an expression of hate. King asserted that to eliminate violence one would have to eliminate hate. He stated, "At the center of non-violence stands the principle of love." King's belief in the interdependent nature of life influenced his thinking that all human life is sacred and interrelated. Therefore, the act of taking a human life is tantamount to committing personal suicide.

King asserted violent conflict resolution would ultimately lead to mankind's co-annihilation. He argued:

> If you succumb to the temptation of using violence in the struggle, unborn generations will be the recipients of a long and desolate night of bitterness, and your chief legacy to the future will be an endless reign of meaningless and chaos.

King believed in prophetic stewardship grounded in the *ethic of courage* and the *ethic of love*. Both recognize, according to King, the interconnectedness and interrelatedness of humanity. This belief, led King to state, "to the degree that I harm my brother, no matter what he is doing to me, to the extent I am harming myself."

From this perspective, there is no such thing as justified violence. King believed the only weapon at man's disposal to fight injustice is nonviolence because it is rooted in the *ethic of love*, which aligns with God's spiritual laws and moral principles. He stated:

> Nonviolence is a powerful and just weapon, which cuts without wounding and ennobles the man who wields. It is a sword that heals.

> I believe that unarmed truth and unconditional love will have the final word in reality. That is why right, temporarily defeated, is stronger than evil triumphant.

King believed in the "affirmation of peace" and that "love is our great instrument and our great weapon, and that alone." Through *the ethic of love* and nonviolent protest, he articulated a moral vision of conflict resolution in which hate, and aggression would be redirected towards consideration for opposing viewpoints. He stated:

> Compassion and nonviolence help us to see the enemy's point of view, to hear his questions, to know his assessment of ourselves. For from his view we may indeed see the basic weaknesses of our own condition, and if we are mature, we may learn and grow and profit from the wisdom of the brothers who are called the opposition.

The *ethic of love*, according to King, is not an excuse for inactivity when confronted with social injustices. He viewed passivity in the face of brutal oppression just as repugnant as violence in response to the same. King was a strong advocate of social protest powered by faith in God which he believed leads to courageous leadership. King's social activism contrasted starkly with traditional methods of protest, which typically include hate, revenge, retaliation, rioting, and violent revolution. He discouraged the use of hate and violence as methods of protest:

> I can't make myself believe that God wants me to hate. I'm tired of violence. And I'm not going

to let my oppressor dictate to me what method I must use. We have power, power that can't be found in Molotov cocktails, but we do have a power. Power that cannot be found in bullets and guns, but we have a power. It is a power as old as the insights of Jesus of Nazareth and as modern as the techniques of Mahatma Gandhi.

Engaging in open, honest, critical dialogue represents a key component of King's servant leadership philosophy. Individuals and groups engaged in conflict, King noted, must be willing to forego narrow thinking, hateful sentiments, violent aggression, and ego to take part *in courageous conversations* on issues negatively impacting society. It takes courage to listen to the opposition; it takes greater courage to admit when the opposition has made a valid point.

Violent conflict resolution, according to King, was both impractical, given the military power of the oppressors, and immoral, given the co-annihilation brought about by warfare. King argued:

> Violence as a way of achieving racial justice is both impractical and immoral. It is impractical because it is a descending spiral ending in destruction for all.

King believed violence would ultimately lead to a "never-ending reign of chaos." He argued:

> I am convinced that if we succumb to the temptation to use violence in our struggle for freedom, unborn generations will be the recipients of a long and desolate night of bitterness, and our chief legacy to them will be a never-ending reign of chaos.

He further stated:

> The old law of an eye for eye leaves everybody blind. It is immoral because it seeks to humiliate the opponent rather than win his understanding; it seeks to annihilate rather than to convert. Violence is immoral because it thrives on hatred rather than love. It destroys community and makes brotherhood impossible. It leaves society in monologue rather than dialogue. Violence ends by defeating itself. It creates bitterness in the survivors and brutality in the destroyers.

A consistent theme in the servant leadership philosophy of King is the desire to transform the "internal violence of the spirit" found society. King correctly pointed out the immorality of violence because, as he stated, violence "thrives on hatred rather than love." He wanted society to courageously engage in critical self-examination to see that violence is the presence of hate and the absence of love.

For King, "nonviolence" is the "affirmation of love." In his numerous sermons King mentioned how nonviolent resistance requires more courage than violent resistance. It is insightful to examine King's understanding of courage and nonviolent resistance within the context of contemporary social action. As stated previously, King's faith in God did not lead to passivity. He did not believe in reliance on God in absence of human agency. King emphasized this point when he stated:

> We must learn that to expect God to do everything while we do nothing is not faith but superstition.

He believed without human agency, the struggle against oppression was impossible.

Throughout King's writings, sermons, public speeches, he consistently called for the oppressed to actively resist their oppression. He stated: "This is no time for apathy or complacency. This is a time for vigorous and positive action." King did not believe in the inevitability of change without human agency.

Change does not roll in on the wheels of inevitability but comes through continuous struggle. And so, we must straighten our backs and work for our freedom. A man can't ride you unless your back is bent.

Human agency, according King, is a critical component of nonviolent resistance. The oppressed must be willing to struggle, sacrifice, suffer, and even die in the fight to end social oppression. To this end, King asserted, "Freedom is never voluntarily given by the oppressor; it must be demanded by the oppressed." And, demanding freedom from a violent oppressor takes courage.

King asserted nonviolent resistance was capable of transforming America and would ultimately lead to the conversion of the entire world. Consequently, King believed in the ultimate triumph of good over evil; he believed in social justice and the inevitable demise of injustice. Although he acknowledged the spiritual and moral shortcomings of humanity, King, nevertheless, exhibited a strong belief in mankind's ability to self-correct and choose a righteous course of action. He challenged all people of goodwill to engage in various forms of nonviolent protest:

It is a time for all people of conscience to call upon America to return to her true home of brotherhood and peaceful pursuits. ... We must demonstrate, teach, and preach, until the very foundations of our nation are shaken. We must work unceasingly to lift this nation that we love to a higher destiny, to a new plateau of compassion, to a more noble expression of humanness.

Servant leaders are courageous leaders. Only "self-assertive manhood," as stated by King, will emancipate marginalized people from the throngs of social injustices. Servant leaders can learn from King's moral vision and use of *ethic of courage* and *ethic of love* to challenge and resist social oppression.

Chapter 5: Care

Injustice anywhere is a threat to justice everywhere. We are caught in an inescapable network of mutuality, tied in a single garment of destiny. Whatever affects one directly, affects all indirectly.

Care is fundamental to servant leadership. Leaders are 'care workers' who apply their leadership knowledge and skills to end social injustice; to build the Beloved Community; to uplift the man farthest down; and to courageously confront oppression and other 'isms' enslaving the human spirit and body. It's impossible to lead others without a deep and abiding care.

Sadly, we live in an uncaring world where the rights of men are trampled upon and disregarded with impunity. As a result, social relations are characterized by suspicion, distrust, anxiety, selfishness, and disloyalty. Is caring a universal human attribute? If so, why do we care so little? Part of the problem is a significant number of people feel that certain people are insignificant and unimportant. And this feeling of not counting contributes to more and more people being "me-centered" or looking for compensatory ways to feel as if they count in the world. King stated:

> Everybody wishes to love and to be loved. He who feels that he is not loved feels that he does not count. Much has happened in the modern world to make men feel that they do not belong.

For King, the *ethic of care* is critically important to leadership practices. He believed love and mutual affection between people as the first step to the reclamation of human dignity and self-respect. He also felt the "me-centered" characteristics of society to be symptomatic of a deeper, far graver problem. People suffer from a superiority-complex or what King described as an "ego-driven desire to be superior to others."

This neurotic desire for superiority, King asserted, is at the heart of uncaring social policies and legislation. King stated a superiority complex accounts for leaders' deeming certain racial groups, countries, religions as inferior and, thereby, unworthy of respect, consideration, and inclusion. Social injustice is the chief outcome of a society overrun by a superiority-complex.

Linking superiority-complex to social injustice explains why King believed social oppression was not only an economic and political issue; but also, a problem rooted in the absence of spirituality, morality, and social conscience. Social injustice, according to King, is an expression of a neurotic, uncaring mindset. For example, impoverished conditions in America's urban centers are ignored because those in the position to do something about it blame the poor for being poor. Instead of examining poverty within the context of draconian economic policies, the poor is accused by elected officials and corporate leaders as lacking worth ethic and initiative.

The first step to solving poverty, King believed, is to see the poor as human beings with dignity, worth and value. He believed the mistreatment of the poor is due to the narrow-mindedness of uncaring, "me centered" leaders. He stated:

> The real tragedy of such narrow provincialism is that we see people as entities or merely things. To seldom do we see people in their humanness. ... We fail to think of them as fellow human beings made from the same basic stuff as we, molded in the same divine image.

King stressed the need for "other-centered" leaders who would put the cares and needs of the poor and other marginalized at the top of their social agenda. He stated in numerous sermons and speeches that establishing the "Beloved Community" required 'other-centered" leadership. King asserted:

> I believe that what self-centered men have torn down, other-centered men can build up.

Being "other-centered" means allocating resources towards helping society's most vulnerable citizens achieve their human potential. Helping the weakest members of society, according to King, is the ultimate expression of care; and the definitive demonstration of social justice.

In contrast, "me-centered" leader view poverty as an inconvenience; it is a visual disturbance taking away from their enjoyments of wealth and prosperity. This view of poverty explains social policies designed to make the poor invisible. Instead of working to develop solutions to end poverty, "me-centered" leaders attempt to mask its presence.

Poverty, for the "other-centered" leader is a social disease requiring immediate remedy. As King stated:

> God never intended for one group of people to live in superfluous inordinate wealth, while others live in abject deadening poverty.

King used his public platform to highlight both domestic and global poverty. During the delivery of his Nobel Peace Prize address, King stated the following regarding poverty:

> A second evil which plagues the modern world is that of poverty. Like a monstrous octopus, it projects it's nagging, prehensile tentacles in lands and villages all over the world. Almost two-thirds of the peoples of the world go to bed hungry at night. They are undernourished, ill-housed, and shabbily clad... So, it is obvious that if a man is to redeem his spiritual and moral "lag," he must go all out to bridge the social and economic gulf between the "haves" and the "have nots" of the world. Poverty is the most urgent item on the agenda of the modern life.

Poverty, from King's perspective, was not only an issue of socioeconomic injustice; it is an issue of humanity's "spiritual and moral lag," or what he aptly defined as "poverty of the spirit." The people in power, the people with the resources to alleviate poverty simply do not care enough about the people living in economic misery. As King stated:

There is nothing new about poverty. What is new, however, is that we have the resources to get rid of it."

In a nation with astonishing material wealth, King advocated for "an all-out world war against poverty" and exhorted America to use her "vast resources of wealth to develop the underdeveloped, school the unschooled, and feed the unfed." These actions, according to King, would serve as evidence as to whether a nation truly has compassion and care for the "least of these." He viewed poverty as a curse with dire consequences for any rich nation that failed to address economic injustice. He argued:

> The curse of poverty has no justification in our age. It is socially cruel and blind as the practice of cannibalism at the dawn of civilization, when men ate each other because they had not yet learned to take food from the soil or to consume the abundant animal life around them. The time has come for us to civilize ourselves by the total, direct, and immediate abolition of poverty.

King equated the failure of rich nations to abolish poverty with being uncivilized. Although King directed criticism at the "hideous poverty" present in underdeveloped nations, he distressingly condemned the United States for failing to solve domestic poverty. He argued:

> America is going to hell if we don't use her vast resources to end poverty and make it possible for all of God's children to have the basic necessities of life.

King had faith in his country. Yet, despite America's professions of good intentions to alleviate the suffering of the poor, King remained skeptical.

Centuries of hard lessons taught Blacks leaders to doubt America's commitment to changing the material condition of Blacks. King's suspicions were rooted the stark reality of that American leaders simply did not care enough about its marginalized citizens. King attempted to draw attention to this fact by speaking on the unity of the human family. He stated:

> We are tied together in the single garment of destiny, caught up in an inescapable network of mutuality.

This network of mutuality, King noted, means "shared experience." Therefore, King asserted, poverty is a shared experience—even if leaders choose to ignore its existence or pass social policies to make it invisible to the affluent.

King's corpus of sermons, speeches, interviews, and other public and private conversations illustrate his commitment to caring leadership. He did not simply proclaim moral conclusions. The evil of poverty was evident to those who experienced as it was to those who cared enough to see it through the eyes of those victimized by economic deprivation.

The *ethic of care*, King noted, requires a solid belief in *agape or* divine love. Divine love uplifts the majesty and sacredness of the human personality. In other words, cathartic railing against the sins of poverty accomplishes little to provide hungry brethren with daily bread.

To eliminate poverty, King believed mankind would have to acknowledge the sacredness of all of humanity. Poverty was not purely a Black issue, although racialized poverty posed a serious challenge because of the intersection of racial discrimination and economic oppression. King understood the implications of poverty from both a domestic and international perspective as threatening national and world peace. He stated:

Now let me say, the next thing we must be concerned about if we are to have peace on earth and good will toward men is the nonviolent affirmation of the sacredness of all human life. Every man is somebody because he is a child of God.

The *ethic of care* begins with acknowledgment of the sacredness of humanity and recognition of man's identity within the spiritual, moral, and intellectual essence of God. As such, every human being is worthy of care and consideration because every human being, as stated by King, is "a child of God."

King challenged America to *collective reflection* on the status of its disinherited citizens. This idea of *collective reflection* was to prompt clarity around issues of poverty and to stimulate vigilant opposition to the forces creating dispossessed communities across America. In other words, King desired reflection on the causes of poverty and social action to fix the problem.

King brought fresh eyes to White America's alternate reality. He chastised America for believing it could maintain its status as the *Greatest Country on Earth* while at the same time condemning a significant number of her citizens to a life of wretched poverty. King called attention to the moral hypocrisy of thinking such. He wanted America to live up to the biblical standard of genuine brotherhood.

But, despite the efficacy of King's moral vision and his call for caring leadership, he concluded that America was unwilling to abandon its elitist agenda. King's message of inclusiveness and care for those on the fringes economically fell on deaf ears. In King's judgement, America was in desperate need of a new kind of leadership and he described the type of leadership needed:

> We need leaders not in love with money but in love with justice. Not in love with publicity but in love with humanity. Leaders who can subject their particular egos to the pressing urgencies of the great cause of freedom. God give us leaders. A time like this demands great leaders. Leaders whom the fog of life cannot chill, men whom the lust of office cannot buy. Leaders who have honor. Leaders who will not lie. Leaders who will stand before a pagan god and damn his treacherous flattery.

King eloquently articulated how the *ethic of care* influences the leadership practices of the servant leader when he stated,

> Life's most persistent and urgent question is, 'What are you doing for others?

In making the point about leadership and the *ethic of care*, King stated if the Beloved Community is to ever become a living reality, America must produce the right kind of leaders. And, the right kind of leaders possess spiritual values, moral principles, and social conscience. This type of leader can lift the nation above what King described as the "narrow confines of individualistic concerns" and into "a broader concern for humanity."

> I would like to suggest something that we must do to live in this world, to prepare to live in it, with the challenges that confront us. The first thing is that we must rise above the narrow confines of individualistic concerns, with a broader concern for humanity. You see, this new world is a world of geographical togetherness. No individual can afford to live alone.

"Me-centered" leaders are uncaring leaders. In contrast with servant leaders, they are in love with money, status, position, and publicity. They are incapable of genuinely caring for humanity. Their leadership style and decisions are ego-driven, resulting in verdicts that are incompatible with brotherhood, positive human relations and, in some cases, morality and ethics.

King described "me-centered" leaders as hardhearted:

> The hardhearted person never truly loves. He engages in a crass utilitarianism which values other people mainly according to their usefulness to him. He never experiences the beauty of friendship, because he is too cold to feel affection for another and is too self-centered to share another's joy and sorrow. He is an isolated island. No outpouring of love links him with the mainland of humanity.

King's legacy provides servant leaders with a model of the *ethic of care*. As the social implications of deepening faith in God gripped King's mind and spirit, he was led to identify racism, poverty, and warfare as the plagues of society. Throughout his career, King articulated a view of how these three diseases warped the human personality, violated human sacredness, and thrust society into chaos.

Chapter 6: Commitment

The hottest place in Hell is reserved for those who remain neutral in times of great moral conflict.

What is commitment? Commitment is consecration of duty—plain and simple. King advocated consecration of duty to fight against social injustices as mandatory for anyone calling themselves a leader. When the *ethic of commitment* is present in the servant leader, sympathy and compassion for the downtrodden is roused.

Dr. Benjamin E. Mays, King's mentor and friend, mentioned a Morehouse man's duty is to do something "for the man farthest down." Who is "the man farthest down," and what are his needs? For King, "the man farthest down" is the world's disinherited. King suffered mental anguish from the lack of opportunities experienced by Black people because of racism and poverty. He understood if racist and the economic-elite were committed to socioeconomic injustices, Black social mobility and access to valued societal resources would be limited.

Disenfranchised groups need inexhaustible service and goodwill to escape the social injustices imprisoning them to ignorance, illiteracy, crime violence, homelessness, joblessness, discrimination, prejudice and, most searing, hopelessness. King acknowledged the power of hopelessness in stifling initiative and resourcefulness in oppressed groups. He stated, "We must accept finite disappointment, but never lose infinite hope." King never viewed societal ills as permanent. He believed "the arc of the moral universe is long, but it bends towards justice." In other words, oppressed groups would eventually experience an end to injustice. King stated:

> Even in the inevitable moments when all seems hopeless, men know that without hope they cannot really live, and in agonizing desperation they cry for the bread of hope.

But the end of injustice and the establishment of the Beloved Community requires human agency because, according to King, God helps those who help themselves. King asserted:

> Every step toward the goal of justice requires sacrifice, suffering, and struggle; the tireless exertions and passionate concern of dedicated individuals.

Hope without active human agency only tightens the chains of oppression. King stated:

> There is little hope for us until we become toughminded enough to break loose from the shackles of prejudice, half-truths, and downright ignorance.

Throughout King's sermons, writings and public speeches, he emphasized the importance of human agency in the fight against social injustices.

> Softminded leaders are not moved— spiritually, emotionally, intellectually or financially—to do anything to help ameliorate poverty and other forms of social injustice. This type of leader is apt to blame the ignorant for being ignorant; the illiterate for being illiterate; the jobless for being jobless; the poor for being poor; and the homeless for being homeless.

> Leaders of this type are barren of humility, lacking in compassion, and unsympathetic towards the marginalized. Arrogance blinds this type of leader from seeing the absurdities of his or her actions. They are silent on the things that matter; King called this type of leadership a "dead leadership." King reminded America that responding to social ills, such as poverty, with silence is tantamount to spiritual and physical death. He stated, "Our lives begin to end the day we become silent about the things that matter."

Not surprisingly, servant-leaders believe serving the needs of the downtrodden is necessary for the advancement of humanity, and that their acts of service are equivalent to worshipping God. Their *ethic of commitment* obligates them to serve as a catalyst for social change. For example, King stated how he wanted to be used by the creator in service to the downtrodden of humanity. He prayed:

> Use me, God, show me how to take who I am, who I want to be, and what I can do, and use it for a purpose greater than myself.

King consistently emphasized the power of human agency in the fight against injustices. His concept of divine intervention consisted of God working through human beings to eliminate social oppression. Therefore, King asserted the need for the oppressed to become active agents in their emancipation from socioeconomic bondage:

> Somewhere we must come to see that human progress never rolls in on the wheels of inevitability. It comes through the tireless efforts and the persistent work of dedicated individuals who are willing to be coworkers with God. And without this hard work, time itself becomes an ally of the primitive forces of social stagnation. So we must help time and realize that the time is always ripe to do right.

King believed committed leadership can change the world. But, unfortunately, few people have genuine sympathy and compassion for the dispossessed; even fewer believe it is their sacred duty to do something about racism or poverty. And, even fewer have the commitment necessary for a long-term fight to end social injustice. There is silence on political agendas rooted in racism, materialism, militarism. There are many Americans who believe something needs to be done about these problems. But they are afraid to speak out. King warned those who choose to remain silent on issues of social injustice:

> In the end we will remember not the words of our enemies but the silence of our friends.

> History will have to record that the greatest tragedy of this period of social transition was not the strident clamor of the bad people, but the appalling silence of the good people

> We will have to repent in this generation not merely for the vitriolic words and actions of the bad people, but for the appalling silence of good people.

King used the idea of silence to illustrate the inaction of people in confronting social injustices. To achieve social justice, King asserted, requires human agency. Servant leaders, according to King, are the *prophetic voice of the voiceless*. One of the greatest expressions of King's commitment to social change was his belief that direct action was authorized by God. He believed there comes a time when direct action against injustice is not only necessary but mandated by the God. King asserted:

> Our only hope today lies in our ability to recapture the revolutionary spirit and go out into a sometimes-hostile world declaring eternal hostility to poverty, racism, and militarism.

To carry out King's vision of leadership with revolutionary spirit, servant leaders are called to resist all forms of social oppression. King asserted, "One has a moral responsibility to disobey unjust laws." According to this perspective, leaders who fail to challenge injustices, including legal injustices, are co-conspirators with those who practice explicit oppression. King's ultimate meaning and significance is that he represented like his mentor, Dr. Benjamin E. Mays, spiritual, intellectual, and social rebellion against social injustice. When servant leaders show the *ethic of commitment* at this level, he or she receives support from God. King asserted how God is the only support needed by servant leaders.

> The God whom we worship is not a weak and incompetent God. He is able to beat back gigantic waves of oppositional and to bring low prodigious mountains of evil. The ringing testimony of the Christian faith is that God is able.

The *ethic of commitment* begins with assurance that one's actions will ultimately lead to success no matter how hard and difficult the struggle; and no matter the obstacles and barriers one encounters.

Commitment is to leadership what health is to the body. Leaders cannot do anything substantial without the *ethic of commitment*. In the mass of historical literature, there is not a class of men as difficult to manage or control as those committed until death to ending social injustice.

King would say the time in which we live demands this type of leader—committed leaders. He would undoubtedly extol the virtues of leaders committed to serving the pressing needs of society. And, he would admonish leaders who served as figure-heads for political-interest groups; leaders who represent the narrow agenda of a political party; and leaders who catered to the interest of the economic-elite. He would stress the necessity for leaders with the ability to assess the needs of society and generate solutions, mold consensus, and then implement constructive programs to improve the quality of life for all Americans. King demonstrated in his leadership an understanding of the responsibilities and demands inherent in servant leadership. Reflecting on the *ethic of commitment*, he stated the following:

> One cannot be in my position, looked to by some for guidance, without being constantly reminded of the awesomeness of its responsibility. I live with one deep concern: Am I making the right decisions? Sometimes I am uncertain, and I must look to God for guidance. ... I subject myself to self-purification and to endless self-analysis; I question and soul-search constantly into myself to be as certain as possible that I am fulfilling the true meaning of my work, that I am maintaining my sense of purpose, that I am holding fast to my ideals, that I am guiding my people in the right direction. But whatever my doubts, however heavy the burden, I feel that I must accept the task of helping to make this nation and this world a better place to live in—for all men, black and white alike.

Probably the most important ingredient in servant leadership is the *ethic of commitment*. Because social injustice is deeply embedded in the psyche and social framework of America, it's difficult to uproot. As a result, King spiritually prepared himself for a protracted struggle against social injustice. He committed his entire life to the struggle for civil rights and the fight to end poverty.

King is arguably the most ardent example of the *ethic of commitment*. One way to understand King's leadership commitment is to view it as giving *prophetic voice to the voiceless*. He spoke for those who lacked voice or whose voices were silenced as result of fear. King noted:

> Never forget that you are where you are today because the masses have helped you get there and they stand now out in the wilderness, not being able to speak for themselves, they stand walking the streets in protest just not knowing what to do and the techniques. They are waiting for somebody out in the midst of the wilderness of life to stand up and speak and take a stand for them.

King knew from experience the simplest way to control people is to silence their voices. The silencing of the disinherited, King argued, will result in the voiceless finding other means to be heard.

> I contend that the cry of 'Black Power' is, at bottom, a reaction to the reluctance of white

power to make the kind of changes necessary to make justice a reality for the Negro. I think that we've got to see that a riot is the language of the unheard. And, what is it that America has failed to hear? It has failed to hear that the economic plight of the Negro poor has worsened over the last few years.

According to King, Black life is a stressful world, filled with racial biases and economic injustices. Yet, more importantly, and most stifling to Black life is their voiceless existence and the unwillingness of American leadership to hear their concerns.

These conditions [racism and poverty] are the things that cause individuals to feel that they have no other alternative than to engage in violent rebellion to get attention. ... Large segments of white society are more concerned about tranquility and the status quo than about justice and humanity.

King came to view poverty as America's greatest social ill. This is truly remarkable given the efficacy of racism to frame social criticism during the 1960s. King's commitment to ending social injustice pushed his leadership thinking beyond criticism of racial segregation as an isolated expression of social oppression. Instead, he perceptively saw how racism and social oppression intersected in ways to serve Whites' economic interest. Whites, according to King, were invested in maintaining the racial status quo because it benefited them economically and socially to do so.

When King assumed leadership of the Civil Rights Movement in the 1955, ending segregation was at the forefront of his moral vision. Ten-plus years later, King's commitment expanded to include poverty as a primary target for social action. His *ethic of commitment* evolved as the Civil Rights Movement morphed into the Poor People's Campaign.

King was a very reflective leader and it dawned on him how poverty, in general, and racialized poverty specifically was the reason for urban rebellions. After his memorable "I Have a Dream" speech of 1963, King's servant leadership perspective grew. While still committed to eradicating racial discrimination to pave the way for Blacks' integration into American society, King's strongest criticism was now directed at what his mentor, Dr. Benjamin E. Mays called America's "sacred cow." He spoke out against America's involvement in the Vietnam War. At the time of his death, King had become an outspoken critic of economic inequality and poverty. At this juncture in his career, King was no longer a popular leader; he was a pariah because of his outspoken criticism of American racism, poverty and warfare.

Despite the political backlash causing a decline in his popularity, King remained committed to belief in the immorality of both poverty and warfare. His moral vision expanded from civil rights to economic injustice. On the issue of poverty, King stated the following a month before his assassination:

> Yes, we are going to bring the tired, the poor, the huddled masses ... We are coming to demand that the government address itself to the problem of poverty.

In a moment of reflection on the vast surplus of food stored in America while families in urban ghettos went to bed hungry, King stated the following:

> I started thinking about the fact that right here in our country we spend millions of dollars every day to store surplus food. And I said to myself: "I know where we can store that food free of charge—in the wrinkled stomachs of the millions of God's children in Asia, Africa, Latin America, and even in our own nation, who go to bed hungry at night.

King was committed to not only ending racial segregation, but also to eradicating the socioeconomic barriers preventing Blacks and the poor from decent jobs, adequate housing, access to health care, and quality education. King challenged America's ideals of all citizens having a right to life, liberty and the pursuit of happiness when he stated:

> If a man doesn't have a job or an income, he has neither life nor liberty nor the possibility for the pursuit of happiness.

King's *ethic of commitment* pushed him to propose a $30 Billion anti-poverty bill which guaranteed a basic income for all Americans. One month later King was assassinated with many believing his commitment to denouncing, as he stated, the "ugliness of poverty," as the chief cause of his assassination.

Listen to the Beat of the Drum

Chapter 7: Competence

Nothing in the world is more dangerous than sincere ignorance and conscientious stupidity.

Like many Black leaders of his era, King was deeply spiritual, highly educated, and deeply committed to elevating the condition of Black people. His leadership reflects the spiritual, intellectual, ethical, and social discourse of the Black protest tradition. To understand King's servant leadership, one must comprehend the tradition that shaped him.

First and foremost, King was a Baptist minister with a strong belief in God. His indictments of racism and class inequality evolved from his staunch commitment to a moral vision for society, and his devoted adherence to ethical leadership. As King's social competence grew, he became increasingly critical of America's social policies. Responsible society or what King called the "Beloved Community" was accountable for making sure its most vulnerable citizens were able experience economic stability.

Moreover, King asserted the government was responsible for solving the problem of poverty concentrated primarily in America's urban and rural communities.

King's mobilization of the masses of impoverished Americans into a Poor People's Campaign was to force the government to make substantive changes to an economic system that produced poverty and protected economic exploitation on the part of a wealthy-elite.

By uniting the poor and disinherited of all races, King hoped to leverage the power of common economic hardship into a social force capable of forcing America to do more for the poor. Racism was still a problem, according to King, but the problem of race intersected with economics, to produce racialized poverty.

Because of the growth and expansion poverty, King believed the "whole structure of American life must change," because poverty was not only a Black issue; upon closer observation, King realized that economic inequality was an issue impacting a large segment of the American population irrespective of race. King's growing social competence pushed him beyond civil rights to demanding a radical distribution of America's wealth.

> We aren't going to Washington to beg, we are
> going to Washington to demand what is ours.

King's *ethic of competence* foreshadowed the class conflicts and war profiteering of contemporary American society. King's forthright denunciation of poverty and warfare, while unpopular to both Blacks and Whites of middle- and -upper classes, resonated with the poor of all races. King saw the folly in not addressing poverty. America was in need—as it is today—of sweeping restructuring of its economic system to solve the problem of mass poverty.

Unfortunately, America's governmental officials and business leaders were unwilling to engage in serious deliberations on America's economic system. King asserted the following regarding the absence of critical thinking skills on the part of today's leadership:

> Rarely do we find men who willingly engage in
> hard, solid thinking. There is an almost universal
> quest for easy answers and half-baked solutions.
> Nothing pains some people more than having to
> think.

Competence, according to King, is more than talent, expertise, aptitude, and skills; it speaks to the centrality of doing what is right – spiritually, morally and ethically. Softminded leaders can be highly skilled, possessors of vast knowledge, with exceptional talents, but lack in spiritual values and moral principles. Their leadership decisions are guided by questions of "Is it safe?"; "Is it politic?"; or "Is it popular" and not "Is it right?" King stated,

> There comes a time when one must take a position that is neither safe nor politic nor popular, but he must take it because conscience tells him it is right.

Competence, according to King, includes also spiritual and moral preparation for sacred duty in the fight to end social injustice. Racism produces hate and a desire for revenge in the hated. Poverty deprives the marginalized of decency and dignity. And, militarism leads to violence, death, and co-annihilation. King boldly stated that racism, materialism, and militarism were social injustices that would plunge the world into violent chaos.

King's concept of "community versus chaos" is derived from his belief in the interconnectedness and interdependence of humanity. His statement, "We must learn to live together as brothers or we will perish together as fools," reflects his belief that individuals and nations who do not act in accordance to human unity are doomed to failure. Hence, the origin of one of King's most popular statements: "Injustice anywhere is a threat to justice everywhere."

King frequently referenced the Gospel of Jesus and with its emphasis on being concerned with the "least of these" as fundamental to servant leadership. The test of leadership, King exhorted, is how leaders respond to the plight of the disposed and marginalized. King never accepted racism, poverty, and warfare as viable practices for organizing society. Although these practices give psychological and material benefit to the few, King purported that all three were social injustices violating the spiritual laws of human interconnected and interdependence.

By the last year of his life, King's leadership philosophy fully matured; it evolved and changed to reflect an understanding of racism as being grounded in economic injustice. When King's leadership expanded beyond the Southern racism to tackling Northern poverty, he quickly grasped the economic scope of white supremacy. Although he understood racism from a spiritual and moral plane, he quickly comprehended its economic dimensions.

King elaborated on the intersection of race, class, economic exploitation when he stated:

> We cannot be satisfied as long as Negro basic mobility is from a smaller ghetto to a larger one.

King understood how race was used to identify Blacks as second-class citizens and how economic inequality was used to make sure they stayed second-class citizens. In other words, economic injustice ensured Blacks would remain poor—at the bottom of the economic ladder. The reality of Blacks' impoverishment in the so-called integrated North led King to assert:

> We are entering deeper night of social disruption in our country; we have the resources to solve our problems. But the question is, do we have the will.

King's *ethic of competence* identified white supremacy, and the laws and social policies derived from this sinister ideology, as the root cause of poverty. He understood ending segregation in law failed to mitigate centuries of economic injustice experienced by Blacks. As King asserted, "Our struggle is for genuine equality, which means economic equality." He went on to say:

> For we know now, that it isn't enough to integrate lunch counters. What does it profit a man to be able to eat at an integrated lunch

counter if he doesn't have enough money to buy a hamburger? What does it profit a man to be able to eat at the swankest integrated restaurant when he doesn't earn enough money to take his wife out to dine? What does it profit one to have access to the hotels of our cities, and the hotels of our highways, when we don't earn enough money to take our family on a vacation? What does it profit one to be able to attend an integrated school, when he doesn't earn enough money to buy his children school clothes?

King recognized he was "treading in difficult waters" by criticizing capitalism and the economic elite. His understanding of the *profit motive* made it highly unlikely America would reverse its course and do something substantive to alleviate racism, eliminate poverty, and lessen the need for warfare. King stated:

> When machines and computers, profit motives and property rights are considered more important than people, the giant triplets of racism, materialism, and militarism are incapable of being conquered.

One benefit to studying the evolving servant leadership philosophy of King is that it provides a blueprint for how leaders can face different kinds of leadership dilemmas. As King's social competency grew, so did his moral vision. His *ethic of competence* challenged him to reinterpret racism as a neurotic disorder causing America to have a superiority complex. King stated America was sick spiritually and morally, and the country's septic addiction to racism, poverty and warfare was the symptom, not the cause. He prophetically stated how America needed a radical change in values and priorities.

Chapter 8: Drum Major Instinct

The drum major instinct can lead to exclusivism in one's thinking and can lead to feel that because he has some training, he's a little better than that person who doesn't have it.

On April 4, 1968, at 6:01 p.m., Dr. Martin Luther King, Jr. was shot and killed while standing on the balcony of the Lorrain Motel, located at 450 Mulberry Street, in downtown Memphis, Tennessee. He was pronounced dead at 7:05 p.m. at the youthful age of 39 years. Two months to the day of his martyrdom, on February 4, 1968, King delivered "I Am a Drum Major for Justice", the last sermon he preached at Ebenezer Baptist Church.

King used the "Drum Major Instinct" sermon to offer a critique of leadership and an inspired vision for living a life of service. Like so many of his speeches and sermons, this one has significant relevance given the contemporary crisis in leadership.

In this sermon, King eloquently outlines the essence of servant leadership and dangers of what he called a "perverted drum major instinct"— a desire to be out front, a desire to lead the parade. King warns his congregation that a desire for superiority can lead to a superiority complex and "tragic race prejudice." King preached on the *drum major instinct* being the root cause of white supremacy.

> Do you know that a lot of the race problem grows out of the drum major instinct? A need that some people have to feel superior … and to feel that their white skin ordained them to be first.

King provided his congregation with a biblical example of how Jesus responded to the *drum major instinct* in His disciples.

According to King, an example of the *drum major instinct* can be found in the request by James and John for a special place in Jesus' kingdom. King preached:

> The setting is clear, James and John are making a specific request of the master. They had dreamed, as most of the Hebrews dreamed, of a coming king of Israel who would set Jerusalem free and establish his kingdom on Mount Zion, and in righteousness rule the world. And they thought Jesus as this kind of king. And they were thinking of that day when Jesus would reign supreme as this new king of Israel. And they were saying, "Now when you establish

> your kingdom, let one of us sit on the right
> hand and the other on the left hand of your
> throne."

The *drum major instinct*, King explained, is a multifaceted attribute, with potential for both good and evil; it is a natural attribute deeply embedded in the psyche of humanity. He went on to explain how Jesus did not admonish John and James for their desire for greatness. Instead of rebuking them as selfishness, Jesus, instead, redirected their desire for greatness from worldly ambition to humble service. As King preached, Jesus "reordered priorities, and encouraged his disciples to "Keep feeling the need to be first. But I want you to be first in love."

King preached how Jesus wanted His disciples to redirect their priorities from selfish, worldly ambition and to love of God, spiritual and moral growth, and service to fallen humanity. The entire dialogue between Jesus and His disciples is a truly remarkable lesson on how to redirect the *drum major instinct*. As King noted:

> ...Let us see that we all have the drum major
> instinct. We all want to be important, to
> surpass others, to achieve distinction, to lead
> the parade.

White supremacy and race prejudice, King explained, are expressions of a "distorted drum major instinct" or what can be defined as an insatiable desire to be superior to others. King described the following:

> There is deep down within all of us an instinct. It's a kind of drum major instinct—a desire to be out front, a desire to lead the parade, a desire to be first. And it is something that runs the whole gamut of life. ...*There comes a time that the drum major instinct can become destructive* [my emphasis].

This explains why King stated that White America needed a transformation in mindset; he stated the need for a new definition of greatness divorced from racial domination and economic exploitation. White America, like James and John, King concluded, need "reordered priorities" and a "new definition of greatness".

> And he transformed the situation by giving a new definition of greatness. And you know how he said it? He said, 'Now brethren, I can't give you greatness. And really, I can't make you first.' This is what Jesus said to James and John. 'You must earn it. True greatness comes not by favoritism, but by fitness. And the

right hand and left hand are not mine to give, they belong to those who are prepared.'

King, drawing on the servant leadership philosophy of Jesus, provides America's leaders a context for understanding white supremacy and white privilege as a "distorted drum major instinct":

> And so, Jesus gave us a new form of greatness. If you want to be important—wonderful. If you want to be recognized—wonderful. If you want to be great—wonderful. But recognize that he who is greatest among you shall be your servant. That's a new definition of greatness...by giving that definition of greatness, it means that everybody can be great, because everybody can serve.

King stated further:

> And this morning, the thing that I like about it [a new norm of greatness]; by giving that definition of greatness, it means that everybody can be great, because everybody can serve. You don't have to have a college degree to serve. You don't have to make your subject and your verb agree to serve. You don't have to know about Plato and Aristotle to serve. You don't have to know Einstein's theory of relativity to serve. You don't have to

> know the second theory of thermodynamics
> in physics to serve. You only need a heart full
> of grace, a soul generated by love. And you can
> be that servant.

Drawing from the servant leadership example of Jesus, King tied greatness to one act: humble service. He challenged White America to "walk in the light of creative of altruism" instead of being chained to white supremacy, which disconnected them from genuine and authentic fellowship with the worldwide community. King stated:

> But this is why we are drifting. And we are
> drifting there because nations are caught up
> with the drum major instinct. 'I must be first.'
> 'I must be supreme.' 'Our nation must rule the
> world.' And I am sad to say that the nation in
> which we live is the supreme culprit. And I'm
> going to continue to say it to America,
> because I love this country too much to see
> the drift that it has taken.

The central thesis of King's sermon is the attainment of greatness through humble service. King's servant leadership philosophy is grounded in the *Gospel of Jesus* which declares service to humanity as the primary goal of leadership. This is

King's most important lesson for leaders. A servant leader is one who forgoes selfishness and works tirelessly to service the needs of God's disinherited children. At the close of his sermon, King shared a message on how he wanted to be eulogized at the close of his earthly mission:

> If any of you are around when I have to meet my day, I don't want a long funeral. ... Tell them not to mention that I have three or four hundred awards. That's not important. Tell them not to mention where I went to school. I'd like somebody to mention that day that Martin Luther King, Jr., tried to give his life serving others. I'd like for somebody to say that day that Martin Luther King, Jr. tried to love somebody. ... I want you to say that I tried to love and serve humanity. Yes, if you want to say that I was a drum major, say that I was a drum major for justice. I was a drum major for righteousness. And all the other shallow things will not matter.

King should be remembered for, as he stated, spreading "the message as the master taught." The message drawn from the life mission of Jesus, according to King, is greatness can be achieved by faith in God and humble service to mankind. We need leaders like King who *listen to the beat of the drum* and stand at the forefront in the fight against social injustice.

50th Anniversary of Dr. Martin Luther King's Death

The sermon King planned to deliver before he was murdered was titled "Why America May Go to Hell". On the morning of his assassination, he planned to deliver this sermon at Ebenezer Baptist Church, the location of his sermon, "The Drum Major Instinct" in 1968. King, with a developed and mature socioeconomic and political outlook, would have delivered a sermon castigating America for her continued pursuit of technological, scientific and military supremacy while ignoring growing poverty. In a prophetic address to the sanitation strikers in Memphis, Tennessee, King provides us with a hint of the sermon he would have delivered that Sunday, April 7, 1968, if he had lived to do so.

> And I come by here to say that America, too, is going to hell if she doesn't use her wealth. If America does not use her vast resources of wealth to end poverty and make it possible for all of God's children to have the basic necessities of life, she, too, will go to hell. And I will hear America through her historians, years and generations to come, saying 'We built gigantic buildings to kiss the skies. We built

gargantuan bridges to span the seas. Through
our spaceships, we were able to carve
highways through the stratosphere. Through
our airplanes, we ae able to dwarf distance and
place time in chains. Through our submarines,
we were able to penetrate oceanic depths.

It seems that I can hear the God of the
Universe saying, 'Even though you have done
all of that, I was hungry and you fed me not. I
was naked and you clothed me not. The
children of my sons and daughters were in
need of economic security and you didn't
provide if for them. And so, you cannot enter
the kingdom of greatness.'

Today, 50 years after King's death, we are
still fighting against racial discrimination,
economic injustice and warfare. King used
prophetic moral vision and nonviolent protest to
compel America to reflect on the socioeconomic
status of its most fragile citizens. His
assassination caused both national mourning and
violent unrest in America's urban centers.
Although King is an icon of nonviolent protest, his
servant leadership philosophy and social activism
is far more complex.

King militantly fought to abolish legalized
racial discrimination; he radically demanded an
end to worldwide poverty; and he forcefully spoke

out against America's involvement in the Vietnam War. King was much more than his "I Have a Dream Speech." King loved America and his moral vision pushed the nation to reexamine the role of white privilege in granting endless opportunities to Whites, while penalizing Blacks via a variety of social and economic proscriptions. King is, arguably, America's greatest leader.

What can today's leaders learn from King's servant leadership legacy? How would King interpret contemporary social problems? What is the impact of King's legacy on America's conscience 50-years after his death? Would the statement that America is going to hell for failing to use her vast resources to remedy poverty resonate today given country's growing and expanding economic inequality?

King believed America's fall or rise is tied to its leadership. In retrospect, King's sermon was a final warning to America's leaders to embrace the principles of servant leadership as the pathway to making America great.

The crowning achievement of King's leadership is the "living template" he provided on how servant leaders respond to leadership dilemmas. They respond, King would attest, by "hewing stones of hope from a mountain of despair."

As we commemorate the 50th anniversary of King's death, servant leaders across the nation are well-advised to reflect on the immortal words of America's fallen solider in the fight against social injustice.

> We must make a choice. Will we continue to march to the drumbeat of conformity and respectability, or will we, listening to the beat of a more distant drum, move to its echoing sounds? Will we march only to the music of time, or will we, risking criticism and abuse, march to the soul saving music of eternity? More than ever before we are today challenged by the words of yesterday, "Be not conformed to this world: but be ye transformed by the renewing of your mind."

REFLECTIONS by
Dr. Martin Luther King, Jr.

Moral principles have lost their distinctiveness.
For modern man, absolute right and absolute
wrong are a matter of what the majority is doing.
...We have unconsciously applied Einstein's
theory of relativity, which properly described the
physical universe, to the moral and ethical realm.

If there is to be peace on earth and good will
toward men, we must finally believe in the
ultimate morality of the universe, and believe that
all reality hinges on moral foundations.

Let us realize that the arc of the moral universe is
long but it bends towards justice.

Our hope for creative living in this world house
that we have inherited lies in our ability to
reestablish the moral ends of our lives in personal
character and social justice. Without this
spiritual and moral reawakening, we shall destroy
ourselves in the misuse of our own instruments.

One of the great problems of mankind is that we suffer from a poverty of the spirit which stands in glaring contrast to our scientific and technological abundance. The richer we have become materially, the poorer we have become morally and spiritually.

We must use time creatively, in the knowledge that the time is always ripe to do right.

Empathy is fellow feeling for the person in need—his pain, agony, and burdens.

I've decided that I'm going to do battle for my philosophy. You ought to believe in something in life, believe that thing so fervently that you will stand up with it till the end of our days.

It may be me crucified. I may even die. But I want it said even if I die in the struggle that, "He died to make men free."

If there is nothing worth dying for, there is nothing worth living for.

A nation or civilization that continues to produce soft-minded men purchases its own spiritual death on the installment plan.

I believe that what self-centered men have torn down, other-centered men can build up.

A genuine leader is not a searcher for consensus but a molder of consensus.

Never forget that you are where you are today because the masses have helped you get there and they stand now out in the wilderness, not being able to speak for themselves. They stand walking the streets in protest just not knowing what to do and the techniques. They are waiting for somebody out in the midst of the wilderness of life to stand up and speak and take a stand for them.

Everybody can be great. Because anybody can serve. You don't have to have a college degree to serve. You don't have to make your subject and your verb agree to serve. You don't have to know Einstein's theory of relativity to serve. You don't have to know the second theory of thermodynamics in physics to serve. You only need a heart full of grace. A soul generated by love.

If any of you are around when I have to meet my day, I don't want a long funeral. ... Tell them not to mention that I have three or four hundred awards. That's not important. Tell them not to mention where I went to school. I'd like somebody to mention that day that Martin Luther King, Jr., tried to give his life serving others. I'd like for somebody to say that day that Martin Luther King, Jr. tried to love somebody. ... And all the other shallow things will not matter. If I can help somebody as I pass along the way, then my living will not be in vain.

We must learn that to expect God to do everything while we do nothing is not faith but superstition.

This is no time for apathy or complacency. This is a time for vigorous and positive action.

Many people fear nothing terribly than to take a position which stands out sharply and clearly from the prevailing opinion. The tendency of most is to adopt a view that is so ambiguous that will include everything and so popular that it will include everybody. Not a few men who cherish lofty and noble ideals hide them under a bushel for fear of being called different.

Oppressed people cannot remain oppressed forever.

The line of progress is never straight. For a period of movement may follow a straight line and then it encounters obstacles and the path bends.

The ultimate measure of a man is not where he stands in moments of comfort and convenience, but where he stands at times of challenge and controversy.

I have no Messiah complex and I know that we may need many leaders to do the job. ... Let us not succumb to divisions and conflicts. The job ahead is too great.

Negroes have straightened their backs in Albany and once a man straightens his back you can't ride him anymore.

The trying of our faith brings forth patience. And when we have been tested, we become mature lacking nothing.

Cowardice asks the question, "Is it safe?" Expediency asks the question, "Is it politic?" But conscience asks the question, "Is it right?" And there comes a time when one must take a position that is neither safe, nor politic, nor popular but because of conscience tells one it is right

Freedom is not free.

Freedom, in the larger and higher sense, every man must gain for himself.

We are entering deeper night of social disruption in our country; we have the resources to solve our problems. But the question is, do we have the will.

We have waited for more than 340 years for our Constitutional and God-given rights.

We cannot be satisfied as long as the Negro basic mobility is from a smaller ghetto to a larger one.

We will not be satisfied until justice rolls down like waters and righteousness like a mighty stream.

A genuine leader is not a searcher for consensus but a molder of consensus.

A lie cannot live.

A man can't ride your back unless it's bent.

A man who won't die for something is not fit to live.

A right delayed is a right denied.

A riot is the language of the unheard.

All labor that uplifts humanity has dignity and importance and should be undertaken with painstaking excellence.

All progress is precarious, and the solution of one problem brings us face to face with another problem.

Almost always, the creative dedicated minority has made the world better.

An individual who breaks a law that conscience tells him is unjust, and who willingly accepts the penalty of imprisonment in order to arouse the conscience of the community over its injustice, is in reality expressing the highest respect for the law.

At the center of non-violence stands the principle of love.

Before the Pilgrims landed at Plymouth, we were here. Before the pen of Jefferson etched across the pages of history the majestic words of the Declaration of Independence, we were here. If the inexpressible cruelties of slavery could not stop us, the opposition we now face will surely fail.

Change does not roll in on the wheels of inevitability but comes through continuous struggle. And so, we must straighten our backs and work for our freedom. A man can't ride you unless your back is bent.

Darkness cannot drive out darkness; only light can do that. Hate cannot drive out hate; only love can do that.

Discrimination is a hellhound that gnaws at

Negroes in every waking moment of their lives to remind them that the lie of their inferiority is accepted as truth in the society dominating them.

Every man must decide whether he will walk in the light of creative altruism or in the darkness of destructive selfishness.

Everything that we see is a shadow cast by that which we do not see.

Faith is taking the first step even when you don't see the whole staircase.

Freedom is never voluntarily given by the oppressor; it must be demanded by the oppressed.

Have we not come to such an impasse in the modern world that we must love our enemies—or else? The chain reaction of evil—hate begetting hate, wars producing more wars —must be broken, or else we shall be plunged into the dark abyss of annihilation.

He who passively accepts evil is as much involved in it as he who helps to perpetrate it. He who accepts evil without protesting against it is really cooperating with it.

History will have to record that the greatest tragedy of this period of social transition was not the strident clamor of the bad people, but the appalling silence of the good people.

Human progress is neither automatic nor inevitable. ... Every step toward the goal of justice requires sacrifice, suffering, and struggle; the tireless exertions and passionate concern of dedicated individuals.

Human salvation lies in the hands of the creatively maladjusted.

I am not interested in power for power's sake, but I'm interested in power that is moral, that is right and that is good.

I believe that unarmed truth and unconditional love will have the final word, in reality. This is why right, temporarily defeated, is stronger than evil triumphant.

I have a dream that my four little children will one day live in a nation where they will not be judged by the color of their skin, but by the content of their character.

I have a dream that one day every valley shall be

exalted, every hill and mountain shall be made low, the rough places will be made straight and the glory of the Lord shall be revealed and all flesh shall see it together.

I have a dream that one day on the red hills of Georgia, the sons of former slaves and the sons of former slave owners will be able to sit together at the table of brotherhood.

I have a dream that one day the sons of former slave owners will be able to sit down together at the table of brotherhood.

I have decided to stick with love. Hate is too great a burden to bear.

I just want to do God's will. And he's allowed me to go to the mountain. And I've looked over, and I've seen the promised land! I may not get there with you, but I want you to know tonight that we as a people will get to the promised land.

I look to a day when people will not be judged by the color of their skin, but by the content of their character.

I refuse to accept the view that mankind is so tragically bound to the starless midnight of racism and war that the bright daybreak of peace and brotherhood can never become a reality. ... I believe that unarmed truth and unconditional love will have the final word.

I submit that an individual who breaks the law that conscience tells him is unjust and willingly accepts the penalty by staying in jail to arouse the conscience of the community over its injustice, is in reality expressing the very highest respect for law.

I submit to you that if a man hasn't discovered something that he will die for, he isn't fit to live.

I want to be the white man's brother, not his brother-in-law.

If a man is called to be a street sweeper, he should sweep streets even as Michelangelo painted, or Beethoven composed music, or Shakespeare wrote poetry. He should sweep streets so well that all the hosts of heaven and earth will pause to say, here lived a great street sweeper who did his job well.

If physical death is the price that I must pay to free my white brothers and sisters from a permanent death of the spirit, then nothing can be more redemptive.

If we are to go forward, we must go back and rediscover those precious values, that all reality hinges on moral foundations and that all reality has spiritual control.

If you succumb to the temptation of using violence in the struggle, unborn generations will be the recipients of a long and desolate night of bitterness, and your chief legacy to the future will be an endless reign of meaningless chaos.

If you will protest courageously, and yet with dignity and Christian love, when the history books are written in future generations, the historians will have to pause and say, "There lived a great people—a black people—who injected new meaning and dignity into the veins of civilization."

In the end, we will remember not the words of our enemies, but the silence of our friends.

Injustice anywhere is a threat to justice everywhere. We are caught in an inescapable network of mutuality, tied in a single garment of destiny. Whatever affects one directly, affects all indirectly.

It is incontestable and deplorable that Negroes

have committed crimes; but they are derivative crimes. They are born of the greater crimes of the white society.

It is not enough to say we must not wage war. It is necessary to love peace and sacrifice for it.

It may be true that the law cannot make a man love me, but it can keep him from lynching me, and I think that's pretty important.

Law and order exist for the purpose of establishing justice and when they fail in this purpose they become the dangerously structured dams that block the flow of social progress.

Life's most persistent and urgent question is, "What are you doing for others?"

Love is the only force capable of transforming an enemy into friend.

Man must evolve for all human conflict a method which rejects revenge, aggression, and retaliation. The foundation of such a method is love.

Never forget that everything Hitler did in Germany was legal.

Never succumb to the temptation of bitterness.

Nonviolence is a powerful and just weapon, which cuts without wounding and ennobles the man who wields it. It is a sword that heals.

Nonviolence means avoiding not only external physical violence but also internal violence of spirit. You not only refuse to shoot a man, but you refuse to hate him.

Nothing in all the world is more dangerous than sincere ignorance and conscientious stupidity.

One of the greatest casualties of the war in Vietnam is the Great Society ... shot down on the battlefield of Vietnam.

One who breaks an unjust law that conscience tells him is unjust, and who willingly accepts the penalty of imprisonment in order to arouse the conscience of the community over its injustice, is in reality expressing the highest respect for law.

Our lives begin to end the day we become silent about things that matter.

Our loyalties must transcend our race, our tribe, our class, and our nation; and this means we must develop a world perspective.

Our scientific power has outrun our spiritual power. We have guided missiles and misguided men.

Peace is not merely a distant goal that we seek, but a means by which we arrive at that goal.

Philanthropy is commendable, but it must not cause the philanthropist to overlook the circumstances of economic injustice which make philanthropy necessary.

Pity may represent little more than the impersonal concern which prompts the mailing of a check, but true sympathy is the personal concern which demands the giving of one's soul.

Property is intended to serve life, and no matter how much we surround it with rights and respect, it has no personal being. It is part of the earth man walks on. It is not man.

Put yourself in a state of mind where you say to yourself, "Here is an opportunity for me to celebrate like never before; my own power, my own ability to get myself to do whatever is necessary."

Rarely do we find men who willingly engage in hard, solid thinking. There is an almost universal quest for easy answers and half-baked solutions. Nothing pains some people more than having to think.

Science investigates; religion interprets. Science gives man knowledge, which is power; religion gives man wisdom, which is control.

Seeing is not always believing.

Shallow understanding from people of good will is more frustrating than absolute misunderstanding from people of ill will.

So, I'm happy tonight. I'm not worried about anything. I'm not fearing any man. Mine eyes have seen the glory of the coming of the Lord!

Take the first step in faith. You don't have to see the whole staircase—just take the first step.

The art of acceptance is the art of making someone who has just done you a small favor wish that he might have done you a greater one.

The first question which the priest and the Levite

asked was: "If I stop to help this man, what will happen to me?" But... the good Samaritan reversed the question: "If I do not stop to help this man, what will happen to him?"

The hope of a secure and livable world lies with disciplined nonconformists who are dedicated to justice, peace, and brotherhood.

The hottest place in Hell is reserved for those who remain neutral in times of great moral conflict.

The limitation of riots, moral questions aside, is that they cannot win and their participants know it. Hence, rioting is not revolutionary but reactionary because it invites defeat. It involves an emotional catharsis, but it must be followed by a sense of futility.

The means by which we live have outdistanced the ends for which we live. Our scientific power has outrun our spiritual power. We have guided missiles and misguided men.

The moral arc of the universe bends at the elbow of justice.

The Negro needs the white man to free him from his fears. The white man needs the Negro to free him from his guilt.

The Negro's great stumbling block in the drive toward freedom is not the White Citizens Councilor or the Ku Klux Klanner but the white moderate who is more devoted to order than to justice.

The past is prophetic in that it asserts loudly that wars are poor chisels for carving out peaceful tomorrows.

The quality, not the longevity, of one's life is what is important.

The question is not whether we will be extremists, but what kind of extremists we will be. ... The nation and the world are in dire need of creative extremists.

The sweltering summer of the Negro's legitimate discontent will not pass until there is an invigorating autumn of freedom and equality.

The time is always right to do what is right.

The ultimate measure of a man is not where he stands in moments of comfort and convenience, but where he stands at times of challenge and controversy.

There is nothing more tragic than to find an individual bogged down in the length of life, devoid of breadth.

We are not makers of history. We are made by history.

We may have all come on different ships, but we're in the same boat now.

We must accept finite disappointment, but never lose infinite hope.

We must build dikes of courage to hold back the flood of fear.

We must concentrate not merely on the negative expulsion of war but the positive affirmation of peace.

We must develop and maintain the capacity to forgive. He who is devoid of the power to forgive is devoid of the power to love. There is some good in the worst of us and some evil in the best of us. When we discover this, we are less prone to hate our enemies.

We must learn to live together as brothers or perish together as fools.

We who in engage in nonviolent direct action are not the creators of tension. We merely bring to the surface the hidden tension that is already alive.

We will have to repent in this generation not merely for the vitriolic words and actions of the bad people, but for the appalling silence of the good people.

We will remember not the words of our enemies, but the silence of our friends.

Whatever your life's work is, do it well. A man should do his job so well that the living, the dead, and the unborn could do it no better.

Yes, I see the Church as the body of Christ. But, oh! How we have blemished and scarred that body through social neglect and through fear of being nonconformists.

Listen to the Beat of the Drum

About the Author

Rashid Faisal, M.Ed., Ed.M., is an educator, public speaker, educational consultant, and researcher in African American education. He served as principal of elementary, middle, and secondary schools in metro-Detroit. Currently, he serves as Executive Director of Faculty and Instruction for a public-school academy in Detroit.

Born in Detroit, Michigan, Faisal completed undergraduate degrees in Sociology, English and Elementary Education at Madonna University. He later completed an MA in Education and Reading through the Rackham School of Graduate Studies at the University of Michigan and the University of Michigan-Dearborn. Faisal completed a second MA in Organizational and School leadership at Teachers College of Columbia University. He is currently a doctoral student in Urban Education and Leadership at the University of Michigan-Dearborn where he received the 2018 Difference Maker of the Year Award for graduate students and Alumni of the Year Award, becoming the first person in school history to win both awards in the same year.

Faisal is a proud member of the Alpha Phi Alpha Fraternity Inc. and served as a charter member of the Sigma Delta Lambda Chapter located in Southfield, Michigan. Faisal lives in the city of Detroit with his wife, Christie, and his daughter Gabrielle.

Listen to the Beat of the Drum